Angels Around The World

Angels Around The World

Brad Steiger

Sherry Hansen Steiger

FAWCETT COLUMBINE

New York

A Fawcett Columbine Book
Published by Ballantine Books
Copyright © 1996 by Brad Steiger and Sherry Hansen Steiger

All rights reserved
under International and Pan-American Copyright Conventions.
Published in the United States by Ballantine Books,
a division of Random House, Inc., New York,
and simultaneously in Canada
by Random House of Canada Limited, Toronto.

http://www.randomhouse.com

Library of Congress Catalog Card Number: 96-96530

ISBN: 0-449-98369-2

Cover design by Kristine V. Mills
Cover art by Edgar Jerins
Book design by Ruth Kolbert

Manufactured in the United States of America

First Edition: October 1996

10 9 8 7 6 5 4 3 2 1

Millions of angels walk the earth unseen,
both when we sleep and when we wake.
JOHN MILTON

CONTENTS

Contents

Contents

Introduction

Angels—the common link between humans and God in all cultures

There are two angels, that attend unseen
Each one of us, and in great books record
Our good and evil deeds. He who writes down
The good ones, after each action closes
His volume, and ascends with it to God.
The other keeps his dreadful day-book open
Till sunset, that we may repent; which doing,
The record of the action fades away,
And leaves a line of white across the page.

—Henry Wadsworth Longfellow, *"The Golden Legend"*

Throughout the course of human history, communication and guidance from the Divine has been delivered by angels in a variety of ways to multitudes all over planet Earth. Regardless of religion, color, or creed, every human culture has been granted the heavenly gift of angelic intervention.

From the very act of creation and the origins of humankind, angels have served as the cosmic link between humans and God, Allah, the Divine Spirit, the Great Spirit, the Supreme Deity, the All-That-Is—or any of the more than one hundred other names for the Living God.

There are many names for the angels, as well. The word for angel in Sanskrit is *angiras*; in Hebrew, *malakh*, meaning "messenger," or *bene elohim*, for "God's children"; and in Greek, *Hoi Hagioi*, the "Holy Ones." In Arabic, the *malakah* are the celestial beings; in Italian, the *putti* are cherubs; and in India, multiwinged angels or beings are called *Garudas*.

In Muslim texts, every human is guarded by two angels—one taking the day watch, the other, night duty. In addition, these two vigilant guardians record their human's good and bad deeds for Judgment Day. Another Muslim legend refers to the *Hafaza*, guardian angels that are assigned to protect each and every person—two by day and two by night. The Qur'an states that when a person dies, the angel who bends over him asks what good deeds he has sent before him.

The Bible refers to angels as Sons of God, Mediators, and Holy Watchers. In general, their main purpose seems to be to make humans better people. To accomplish this, they advise, rescue, warn, punish, and instruct. They sing and make celestial music, on occasion heralding their approach with trumpets. They are able to speak in many tongues, and whatever their utterances, they make them with power and authority. They can be heard by one or by many—sometimes only as the "still, small voice within." The Bible also states that the angels were made a little higher than humans, yet it depicts some angels as sitting at the feet of God.

In all forms of religious expression throughout the world, angelic beings may appear in dreams by night or in visions by day. They can be visible or invisible. They can be felt as a presence, or can appear as a mist, a haze, a cloud, a pillar of cloud, a pillar of fire, or a burning bush. They can fill a room with light or manifest as a blinding light, a ball of light, or a Light Being. They can come and go in chariots and ride on the wind. They can appear and disappear in the blink of an eye. And sometimes they can even be mistaken for ordinary human beings, acting human enough to knock on a door, dine at a table, or lodge as an overnight guest.

Angels have delivered a people or a nation—but they have also destroyed cities and annihilated entire armies. They have sheltered, rescued, and healed many human supplicants—but they have also directed pestilence and other terrible afflictions.

In all of the world religions, angels seemed most concerned with calling upon all people to examine their souls, to improve their treatment of their fellow beings, to resist passing judgment on others, and to put aside intolerance and prejudice in favor of becoming more loving and forgiving.

It seems likely that representatives from all the many world religions would agree with St. Thomas Aquinas's assessment when he said, "An angel can illumine the thought and mind of man by strengthening the power of vision, and by bringing within his reach some truth which the angel himself contemplates." Within the last decade, angels have once again become recognized by large numbers of ordinary people as our heavenly guides and benefactors. Some theorize this recent angelic activation is due to the approaching millennium. Others suggest that our celestial guardians have become greatly concerned about environmental abuse of the planet. Still others warn that Judgment Day is at hand.

For whatever reasons, hundreds of people have come forward to declare that angels have given them warnings, admonitions, prophetic messages, visions, special assignments, and even physical assistance and financial aid. Thousands of sincere men and women have forthrightly stated their heartfelt belief that angels have provided them with guidance, protection, and assistance in the challenges that they face in life, and that angels have walked beside them through personal crises and times of testing.

MANY THOUGHTFUL SCHOLARS throughout the ages have observed that one of the basic purposes of angels in all forms of religious expression is to help humans understand that they are immortal, that their spirit comes from a divine world—a heavenly, angelic realm—and that it may also return to that higher dimension. Although each earthly religion may have a particular sacred history, a unique language which describes the experience of the holy, as well as its own variety of hymns, rituals, and ecclesiastical forms, all are surprisingly similar in purpose and content. And, of greatest importance now in our ever-shrinking world, all of the sacred teachings relayed by the angelic messengers teach respect and tolerance for other human beings.

Those who read and study for themselves the sacred teachings of all religions will find a golden thread running through every one of them: There is but one Supreme Being that transcends matter and the world of material form, and we may go beyond space and time to touch God's holy essence through a sacred inner experience.

In our research, counseling, lecturing, teaching—stories have been sent to us or told to us. In addition, in response to our questionnaire, people worldwide have sent us their stories. The stories contained in *Angels Around the World* will explore the many ways in which angelic beings manifest to all peoples and all cultures and religions. We pray that our efforts will enlighten you, illuminate your Earth path more clearly, and enable you to distinguish a purpose and a plan in a seemingly chaotic world. We also hope that a pattern will emerge that will profoundly demonstrate that we are all One and that we are all loved by God and the angels.

Our Questionnaire Brings Reports Of Angels Around The World

In *Angels Over Their Shoulders*, we described the questionnaire of mystical and paranormal experiences that we have been sending to readers of our books for nearly thirty years. In addition to answering the survey questions, many men and women who have undergone angelic encounters feel compelled to share additional details of their interaction with heavenly beings.

Here are a few excerpts from those accounts of our readers telling us of angels in action around the world:

Jordan

A woman we'll call Anna Hanke, an administrative assistant from Brooklyn, told of the time that she was riding in an open jeep in Jordan in 1970. She was in the backseat on the left, and a nurse was on the right.

"We were going down a highway when a loud voice yelled at me in English: 'Move!' " Anna told us.

"I was so frightened by this booming voice that I immediately jumped to my left. At that instant a shot rang out, and the nurse was struck and killed. I would have been killed had the bullet hit me instead."

Anna asked the driver if he had yelled to her to move. "Of course not," he said. "I didn't even see the sniper!"

"I know that I have heard that voice before," Anna said. "It was my guardian angel warning me."

Israel

David Rosenfeld wrote to tell of the extraordinary incident that occurred while he was serving in the Israel Defense Forces.

"It would have been a fatal accident while on maneuvers," he told us. "An accident, but nonetheless, I certainly would have been dead."

One of Rosenfeld's fellow soldiers, less than ten feet away from him, accidently discharged his rifle.

"I was literally looking right down the barrel of that rifle. Somehow I knew that the rifle was going to fire."

And then everything went into slow motion.

"It was almost as if it were all happening on a strip of motion picture film and time was advancing frame by frame," he said. "I could see the bullet that was moving toward my head, and somehow, it was moving slowly enough for me to get out of the way."

In the next minisecond, a bright light moved between Rosenfeld and the bullet and pushed him away with a powerful shove.

"As I went sprawling to the ground, I saw that all the other soldiers were frozen into immobility. But as soon as my body struck the earth, everything resumed normal speed. That's when I heard the loud report of the rifle and the bullet as it ricocheted off a rock.

"I know that what I have told you is physically impossible, but if it had not happened just as I have said, I would not be around to tell you about it. I have always believed that I had a guardian angel, and I am certain it was he who appeared as the bright light and pushed me out of harm's way."

France

Nina B. wrote to tell us of the days when she was a dancer at the Lido in Paris and was rescued from a personal attack by an angelic being.

"After many hours as a performer, I would usually be very tired, and I would share a taxi home with two other dancers who lived in the same apartment building," she began her account.

"On this evening, for some reason, I felt like walking for a while through the streets of Paris. It would be dawn in a few hours, and I felt like seeing the sun come up. It seemed as though I had not seen the sunrise for many years."

As Nina walked casually, relaxing, letting herself unwind from the tensions of her performance, she became aware of the sound of footsteps behind her.

"I saw the forms of two men duck into the shadows when I stopped to turn around," she said. "Without really thinking, I had chosen to walk down streets that were not very well lighted. And although Paris is a city that never sleeps, these streets were very empty."

Not wishing to allow her fears to get the better of her, she continued to walk, putting on a small show of great confidence and assurance.

"The footsteps picked up their pace as well," she continued her story. "When I glanced quickly over my shoulder, I saw two young men following me. I could see by their gait that they had been drinking heavily. I became frightened, for I knew that alcohol would interfere with their reason and fire their passions."

Nina began to pray. "As a child I had attended convent school. For a time, my family thought that I might become a nun. If I had not so loved to dance, who knows? That night on that dark and deserted street, I began to wish that I had chosen to become a nun singing in the choir of a convent rather than a dancer in the chorus line of the Lido de Paris."

Nina said that she had always felt the presence of a guardian angel. "As a child, I was certain that I had once heard a chorus of angelic voices, and another time I was positive that I had seen an angel standing watch at my bedside."

Nina was praying for the protection of her guardian angel when the two young men caught up to her and one of them grabbed her arm.

"Their faces looked like the leering masks of demons," Nina said. "They were shouting foul things, and I could see that nothing I would say would matter to them. I began to fear for the worst."

But then suddenly a large, powerfully built man appeared directly behind Nina's assailants.

"He had huge hands, and he slammed their heads together so hard that they fell to their knees, crying out in pain as they rolled over on their backs on the sidewalk.

My protector had taken away all evil thoughts from their minds with one sudden blow."

Nina thanked her rescuer profusely. "He was so plainly dressed that I assumed he must be very poor. I offered him some money, but he refused. I then suggested I buy him a meal, and he just smiled."

Nina was distracted by the sound of a taxi approaching. "I hailed the cab, and when I turned back to insist that my benefactor join me for breakfast, he was gone. I could see him nowhere on the street. It seemed impossible that anyone could have disappeared so quickly.

"But the two young men were beginning to sit up and curse, so I decided that the cab had come along just in time."

Nina got into the cab and was grateful to be able to leave the scene of what could have been a very grim episode in her life.

"I will always believe that Mother Mary heard my prayer and sent a powerful angel to protect me from those two thugs," Nina concluded. "He literally appeared from nowhere and vanished in seconds. And he probably saved my life."

Italy

Today Frank Manzetti runs a small, but successful, import-export business in Rome. According to his account, he owes his good fortune to the timely appearance of an angel.

"I was trying my best to put up a good appearance in order to gain the business support of a number of influential businessmen in Rome," he said, beginning his story. "I had practically no working capital, so I would have to obtain merchandise on credit. Once I had acquired a substantial inventory, I had great confidence that I could be successful as an exporter. As a young man, I had the opportunity to travel a great deal throughout all of Europe and overseas. I had established many good contacts that I knew would pay off if only I could convince enough companies to grant me credit."

On this fateful day in June of 1979, Frank was rushing to return to the small office space that he had rented before he received an important call from a major business contact.

"I was returning from lunch with Mr. Paccione, a small manufacturer, who said that he would extend credit to me if I could also obtain credit from Mr. Galluzzo, who had a much larger company," Manzetti said. "It was from Galluzzo that I was expecting the call. I had asked him to please call me at three o'clock. I planned to tell him that I had secured the credit and the confidence of Mr. Paccione, so would he, please, now also extend his credit to me."

Frank thought that he had allowed more than enough

time to return to his office to take the call, but traffic in the city that day was even worse than usual.

"I had no secretary to answer the telephone. And, of course, in those days there were no answering machines readily available to businessmen with my kind of budget. And even if there were, it would have been in terribly poor taste to have a machine answer such an important call from such an influential person."

Frank had portrayed himself to Galluzzo as a well-established importer-exporter with an extensive inventory and experienced staff.

"I knew that I really would have these things one day soon. I had to live my dream before it had happened for the sake of my wife and three children."

But on the afternoon in June, it appeared that all was lost.

"It was ten minutes to three. There was no way that I could return to the office in less than twenty minutes. The traffic jam would cost me my dream and my future."

Frank looked at his wristwatch. He felt every second that ticked by as if it were a thorn piercing his flesh. He became nauseated. His best business suit was drenched with nervous sweat. Mr. Galluzzo was a stern-faced, no-nonsense businessman in his early sixties. He would not tolerate being asked to call at a certain time and having his call go unanswered. It would be unlikely that he would ever talk to Frank again.

"I arrived back at my office at 3:18. I had missed Galluzzo's call by eighteen minutes. I felt terrible. I didn't know what to do."

A few minutes later, after he had calmed himself to some degree, he felt that he had nothing to lose by calling the man and attempting to explain matters.

When Frank heard the sharp voice of Galluzzo's snappish secretary, he almost hung up the telephone.

"I decided to see it through. When Galluzzo came on the line, I expected his first words to come out in a roar."

Frank Manzetti got the surprise of his life.

"Ah, Frank, you managed to extricate yourself from that terrible traffic jam," Galluzzo began. "It's good to hear your voice. Do you have good news from Mr. Paccione?"

Frank was taken off guard. How did Galluzzo know about the traffic jam and his luncheon meeting with Paccione? He had wanted Galluzzo to believe that his arrangement with Paccione was one that had been well established quite some time ago.

Before Frank could respond, Galluzzo said in a whisper, "You have a fantastic secretary, Frank. What a marvelous voice and such a professional manner. Where did you ever find such a jewel? I'm really quite jealous."

Frank was dumbstruck. Finally he managed to mumble, "You spoke to my secretary?"

Galluzzo chuckled. "Who else would answer your office phone? Yes, she explained that you had called in to say that you were stuck in traffic and would be a few minutes late getting back to the office. She said that you would return my call the minute you got in. Frank, if the rest of your staff is as competent and professional as that young lady, you will have no problem in securing my full confidence and an extension of credit to put things into full operation."

Frank Manzetti was firm in his conclusion: "It could only have been an angel taking pity on me. I had no secretary, no answering service, no answering machine. Yet some very confident 'young woman' with a lovely voice and a professional manner answered my important telephone from Mr. Galluzzo and saved my future for me. There can be no other explanation."

New York

And while we're on the subject of angelic intervention over the telephone line, here is a lovely story that one of our readers sent to us about a woman we'll call Martha Jennings.

Martha Jennings was left with ten dollars to her name when her husband walked out on her, leaving her with a small baby to feed. She had lost her job weeks before. Her unemployment insurance had run out. She owed rent money. Her utilities were about to be shut off.

Martha had been advised to accept welfare, but she just

could not bring herself to do it. She had worked all of her life, and she had never really been in any kind of financial trouble until now.

But then she looked at her baby. How far would ten dollars go toward keeping the child fed?

She despised the idea of accepting a handout, yet she could see no other way.

She picked up her phone and dialed the number of the local welfare office in her area of New York City. She was surprised when the voice on the other end of the line answered with the name of a prominent business firm. She had dialed the wrong number. And the telephone company would probably disconnect her service before she could redial.

Martha could not help herself. She began to cry, and she found herself telling the stranger at the business office that she was destitute.

But Martha had found a sympathetic ear. The woman asked what experience, credentials, and qualifications she had. She immediately spoke to someone in the office, then called Martha about an hour later to say that a position requiring someone of her expertise had just opened.

"Can you come in right away for a job interview?" Martha heard the woman ask.

Martha prevailed on a neighbor to watch her baby, and she was at the firm that afternoon. She is now an executive with the company.

"I'll never believe that I dialed that number by accident," Martha Jennings said. "I know that my guardian angel guided my finger and came to my rescue during my darkest hour."

Argentina

An Angel Brought Ernesto's Spirit to a Final Communion

One of our correspondents from Bahia Blanca, Argentina, sent us a moving account of her cousin Angelica Careaga, who received Communion the day after her husband Ernesto had been laid to rest in August 1990.

Angelica had attended the early Mass that Sunday, and her thoughts were filled with anguish as she contemplated the long years ahead without Ernesto.

She sensed a presence next to her in the pew, kneeling beside her. She *knew* that it was Ernesto, but she did not turn to look. She didn't wish to do anything to destroy the impression that she had of her husband's presence. She wanted desperately to hold on to the feeling that Ernesto had actually returned to attend Mass with her.

When Angelica went forward to receive the sacrament at the altar rail, she felt that the presence of Ernesto walked with her. But after she knelt to receive the wafer, she sensed that her husband had once again left her. She was sad, but she was also heartened to have felt him so near, so strongly.

A few days later, Angelica was visiting with her priest, Father Campos. The priest told her that he had to relate a most unusual occurrence that he had experienced at early Mass that Sunday. "As I was turning to face the altar," he said, "I had the most peculiar feeling that Ernesto had come in and had knelt down beside you in the pew. When you walked to the altar to receive the sacrament, I had to blink my eyes. It seemed as though I could behold a dim outline of Ernesto in the company of an angel standing just behind you."

Concluding her account, our correspondent wrote: "My cousin Angelica received spiritual comfort beyond words to be able to believe that her husband's spirit in the company of an angel had joined her in church that Sunday morning to partake of a farewell Communion service with her."

Australia

SHE WALKED WITH HER PARENTS AND THE ANGELS IN HEAVEN

Katherine Waverley of Canberra, Australia, told us of her experience as a living ghost who journeyed to heaven with angelic beings while she was under the surgeon's knife in the late 1960s.

"When I entered the hospital, I knew that I was much sicker than my doctor had conceded," Katherine stated in her account of her remarkable adventure in the higher dimensions of reality.

"Two young interns saw to prepping me for surgery, and as they discussed their after-work plans, I thought about how marvelous it was to be young and to be able to plan for the future," she said. "I was forty-nine years old, and very ill, and I felt that I had come to the end of my life path."

Katherine remembers being asked to count backwards from one hundred, and then she seemed to be spinning crazily around and around.

"I heard a kind of crackling noise, like stiff paper being crunched up into a ball. Then I seemed to be bobbing like a balloon on a string. Truly, the fairest comparison that I can make is that I was a kind of shining balloon attached to my body by a silver string. I could see my body below me, and the two interns, still chattering away about their plans for the evening.

"Then I could see the surgeon, Dr. Glauser, coming down the hall, taking a last puff on a cigarette before he ground it out in an ashtray filled with white sand. He stood beside me, glanced at me, then looked me over very carefully—and became very angry. He swore at the two interns and shouted at them as if they were small, naughty boys. Nurses came running at his shouts. My body was quickly wheeled into surgery.

"*Oh, no,* I thought. *Something has gone terribly wrong. That's why I'm floating up here above everything. I must be dying.*"

Katherine remembered thinking about her husband Dennis and her two daughters, Wendy and Terry.

"I felt sad. Not for me, but for them."

As if from very far away, Katherine heard her doctor shouting at the staff, but she didn't want to watch what was going on in the operating room.

"I didn't seem to feel any more sickness or pain. I felt, somehow, as if I were finished with all that bother. It wasn't as if I no longer cared what happened to me, but I seemed to be growing more and more indifferent toward the physical me."

Then she heard bells tolling, as they do at funerals. Yes, she thought, she must indeed be quite dead.

But suddenly she heard a deep voice say, *"Not yet!"*

"And I felt myself being pulled upward and upward, like an arrow being shot into the sky!"

The next thing Katherine knew was that she was no longer a kind of shining balloon but seemed once again to be her familiar physical self. Standing before her were a number of figures in bright, glowing robes.

"The beings seemed to glow with an inner radiance," Katherine told us. "To me, they were what angels were supposed to look like, only they didn't have wings."

Katherine stood in awed silence for a moment or two before she spoke: "I am dead, then, aren't I?"

One of the angelic figures answered in a gentle, musical voice. "You may stay here for only a while, dear, then you must go back."

When Katherine remembered the heavenly experience

for the account that she wrote for us, she was certain that she had seen green fields and trees and brooks and streams.

"I recall remarking how beautiful Heaven was—and then at almost precisely the same moment, I reasoned that if I were in Heaven I should be able to see my parents. In a twinkling, Mom and Dad were standing beside me, and we were all weeping tears of joy at our reunion!"

Neither of her parents appeared as old as they had when they died. Instead, Katherine told us, "both of them looked as I remembered them from my late childhood or early teenage years."

In retrospect, it seemed as though she visited with her parents for hours, even days. Then an angel in a white robe came for her and informed her that it was time for her to return.

"No sooner had the angel told me this when I was bobbing up near the ceiling of a hospital room. I was shocked to hear Father Galvin giving me the last rites! My husband and daughters were crying, and my sister Donna was there. A nurse stood at the left side of the bed with her fingers on my pulse."

Once again Katherine heard that same deep voice: *"It is not yet your time!"*

"And I heard that same weird, crackling noise. I saw the color of blood all around me—and I was back in my body!"

Katherine moaned with the pain of the illness and the recently completed surgery. When she opened her eyes, Dennis, Wendy, Terry, Donna, and Father Galvin were smiling at her.

"All the saints and Mother Mary be praised," Father Galvin said. "Our Katy is back among us."

The priest asked the nurse to summon Dr. Glauser to examine her.

As soon as she regained command of her tongue, Katherine told everyone that she had gone to Heaven with the angels and that she had seen her deceased parents.

Later, Katherine learned why no one seemed surprised by her statement. "After the surgery, Dr. Glauser had given me only a few hours to pass the crisis point or to die. Father Galvin had been called by Dennis to administer the last rites, because my chances to live seemed almost nonexistent.

"I know that my experience with the angels in Heaven was genuine," Katherine concluded. "I know that my family believes me, as well."

Austria

*A*NGELS SAVED HIM
FROM THE GESTAPO

Our late friend J. Wolfgang Weilgart first met an angelic being when he was a child of six in his native Austria.

Many years later, with doctoral degrees in linguistics and psychology from the universities of Vienna and Heidelberg, he described for us the mystical moment in his childhood when a stranger in a "star-strewn mantle" appeared to him. It was this angelic visitation, Dr. Weilgart stated, that inspired him to devote his life to a new unity of humankind. In that moment of awe and reverence he felt a "cosmic lifestream" enter him, as if his former life had been dissolved.

When Wolfgang told his parents of his experience, they sent him to a psychiatrist, who found the six-year-old's only abnormality to be the fact that he could solve academic problems at the level of a thirteen-year-old. His Binet IQ tested above 200. The psychiatrist warned Wolfgang that in Western society uncommon experiences may be told only as dreams or in poems.

Later, as a young scholar, Weilgart wrote his first doctoral dissertation on "Creation and Contemplation." His paper was one of the few outspoken pacifist arguments against Hitler and the whole Nazi ideology of aggressive action.

Weilgart's father, Dr. Hofrat Weilgartner, had worked for the *Anschluss* (the annexation of Austria by Germany), and so the Nazis expected similar cooperation from the son. The Nazis offered Weilgart a high position in their secret service because of his fluency in a dozen different languages, his knowledge of psychology, and his friendship with the underground—against whom they wished him to be an informer. But he had received another of his cosmic communications from the angel in the "star-strewn mantle." He spent an afternoon and an evening wrapped in solitary contemplation, seeking guidance from his heavenly advisor. Although a position in the

intelligence corps would have been the only way to reha-
bilitate himself in the eyes of the Nazis, whom he had
offended by his doctoral dissertation, Weilgart refused.

His angelic guide warned him that the Gestapo were
keeping him under close watch. "Flee to Holland at
once," the cosmic voice told him.

Weilgart had few friends whom he could trust, and no
connections with practical helpers. His parents had filled
his pockets with money, but so much cash was a sign of
one who was seeking to flee the country.

Following his inner, angelic voice, he encountered a
stranger near the border whom he felt he could trust. He
gave the man all of his funds, together with his parents'
address, and asked him to send the money to the Weilgartner residence. Although the stranger could have sus-
pected Weilgart of flight, turned him in to the Gestapo,
and kept the money for himself, the man (perhaps an
angel in disguise) did as he had been requested.

As Weilgart approached the border, he encountered a
Gestapo patrol, who were searching everyone who
wished to leave or enter the country. The guard blocked
his path and demanded to see his identity papers. Weilgart
knew that an order to arrest him had been issued by the
Gestapo.

And then, once again, just as had occurred when he was
a boy of six, he felt a "cosmic lifestream" entering his
body. To his great surprise, Weilgart suddenly heard *his*

own voice ordering the Gestapo patrol to leave their station at the border and assume another assignment.

To his astonishment, the patrol obeyed his sharp commands, as if he wore the uniform of a high-ranking officer rather than a rumpled business suit. Without another word, the very Gestapo border patrol that had been assigned to arrest him walked quietly away and allowed him to cross the border without the slightest interference.

Although the scholar made good his flight to Holland, it was not long before that nation was being invaded by the Nazis, who would execute Weilgart as a deserter if they should discover his exact whereabouts.

The young mystic's inner voice brought him to the Dutch governor of Java, who happened to be visiting in The Hague. The governor listened to Weilgart's predicament, then sat down, wrote a visa for him, and presented him with a ship ticket to America. In the meantime, somebody had sent Weilgart's poems to German expatriate Thomas Mann, who, as a Nobel Prize–winner and an honorary doctor at the University of California, was able to arrange for him to receive a postdoctoral research fellowship to write his book *Shakespeare Psychognostic*.

Dr. John Wolfgang Weilgart had at last escaped the Nazi threat to freedom and arrived in the United States, where the mission of peace, love, and brotherhood assigned to him by his angelic guide could receive a much fuller expression.

Canada

SHE RECEIVED
AN ANGELIC DONATION
TO FEED HER HUNGRY GIRLS

"Yes, I believe in miracles, and I believe in angels," Cindy Graham told us. "I had an angel appear and give me fifty dollars so I could feed my daughters."

In the fall of 1992, twenty-nine-year-old Cindy was moving from Edmonton, Alberta, to Toronto, Ontario, with the promise that a cousin could help her find suitable employment. Her husband Dwight had been killed in an automobile accident, and his meager insurance policies had barely provided enough money for a burial.

"I was down to my last few dollars," Cindy told us. "I

just couldn't find the kind of job that would allow me to support my children and still have enough money to get a decent apartment in a good neighborhood. When my second cousin Charlene said that she could find a good job for me, I decided to gamble the last bit of money I had left on a bus trip to Toronto."

Cindy had packed some peanut butter sandwiches and a small bag of potato chips for the bus trip, but they didn't last the three of them very long.

"Margie was only six and Mindy was just four. I couldn't stand it when they would cry because they were hungry. I also knew that they would probably develop motion sickness a lot faster if their little stomachs were empty. It seemed like we had barely started the long bus ride when our food was gone. I promised them I would get them something good to eat at Winnipeg, but I knew that I was down to my last three dollars. I didn't know how we would last all the way to Toronto."

Cindy finally got the girls to sleep after they divided the last half of a peanut butter sandwich.

"There were only a few passengers on board at that point in the trip, but I figured the bus would fill up after the Winnipeg stop. I have never had to beg for anything in my life, but I thought an elderly man sitting toward the back looked kind. I sat quietly for several minutes, trying to get up the courage to ask him for just a few dollars for the girls."

Before she got to her feet to make the humiliating journey to the back of the bus with her mental begging bowl in hand, Cindy began to pray.

"I asked God to have mercy on us. I asked if I could somehow get just enough money to buy the girls a decent meal. I knew Charlene would lend me some money when we got to Toronto, but I had been too ashamed to ask her for any money for the trip. I told God that I just had to have some money. Margie and Mindy would be starved and sick long before we reached our final destination."

By the time she had finished praying, Cindy was crying.

"That's when I felt someone touch me on the shoulder. I turned around to see a beautiful lady all dressed in white. At first her whole body seemed to be outlined with a thin, bright light. Then the light kept growing until she was completely enveloped in this magnificent illumination. Suddenly it seemed as if I were somewhere on a cloud way up in the sky instead of on a bus."

Cindy remembered that the beautiful lady told her not to worry. " 'Your life is going to be so much better now,' she told me. 'You and the girls are going to be just fine. Know that God is good, and we, the angels, keep watch over you always. Know also, that we love you.' "

With those words, the angel disappeared.

"But I had tangible proof that she had been there,"

Cindy said. "A crisp new fifty-dollar bill was sticking out of my blouse pocket!"

Cindy saw that the bus driver seemed to be watching her in the rearview mirror. She wondered if he had seen the angel manifest.

"Is everything all right, ma'am?" he asked.

"Did you see the beautiful lady in white who was standing behind me?" Cindy wanted to know.

The driver shook his head. "No, I surely didn't. There was no lady standing behind you, beautiful or otherwise. But you seemed to be acting strangely, like you were troubled or sick or something."

Cindy smiled broadly. "I was troubled, thank you, sir. But I'm not anymore. I know that God and the angels are looking out for me."

"Glad to hear it," he said, giving her a crooked smile. "Hope they look in on me once in a while, too."

"You can bank on it," Cindy told him, clutching the fifty dollars of Heaven-sent help. When the bus pulled into Winnipeg, she would be able to buy the girls a nice, warm meal. The long trip to Toronto would seem a lot shorter with food in their stomachs. They had been provided for by an angel.

ℰTHEREAL BEINGS SENT HER BACK TO GUIDE OTHERS

In 1966 we made the acquaintance of Malva Dee, an attractive and personable young woman who had developed a reputation as a clairvoyant and who had established her own "enchanted acres" in the beautiful region known as the Haliburton Highlands, about 150 miles northeast of Toronto.

MALVA DID NOT BEGIN to express paranormal talents until 1960, when the normally healthy and vital woman suddenly became gravely ill and was taken to the hospital. She was told that death was very near.

She experienced a month of complete despair. Then one night, she told us, "I beheld a vision of myself walking up a very long red carpet which was laid in a beautiful white marbled and arched cathedral. At the end of this magnificent vaultlike room stood a raised dais upon which sat a white-robed figure surrounded by other ethereal-looking personages.

"A feeling of great peace came over me as I walked steadily forward. Then, suddenly, a mighty voice resounded in the hushed hall: 'Go back, my child. It is not yet your time to come home. There is much that you must do to help others.' "

Within five days, Malva Dee walked out of the hospital completely cured. Her doctors regarded her recovery as a miracle produced by modern medicine, but Malva knew that her remarkable healing had come from a much higher source.

Malva was quick to state that she did not know why the angels chose her to serve her brothers and sisters on Earth, but neither did she question their heavenly will. "I merely do that which comes before me in the faith that my path will ever be so guided."

While Malva built an impressive reputation for helping others through her angelically inspired precognitive and clairvoyant abilities, on numerous occasions her psychic warning system saved her own family from tragedy.

Once, when the family was driving in a large city, Malva was suddenly overcome by a sensation of blood and nameless horror. She insisted that her husband pull over for ten minutes while she waited for her angel to give the all-clear signal.

"All right," she told her husband at last. "We may go again."

Minutes later, they came to a busy intersection where a sports car had rammed a truck. The driver of the car had been killed on impact. Had Malva not insisted upon her husband's pulling over, they would have been involved in the accident.

On another occasion, Malva warned her husband to be on the alert for a white car that would suddenly spin out in front of them as they drove in the city.

Later, while they were driving up a hill, a driverless white car came from nowhere, spinning crazily toward their car and the other vehicles in their lane of traffic. A heroic effort on the part of a bystander—who ran out in the street, jumped into the runaway car, and slammed on the brakes—prevented a deadly toll of damaged vehicles and injured motorists.

MALVA DEE TOLD US that she tried always to proceed through the challenges of life with a calm and peaceful mind. No dour, pessimistic prophet, she believes that the future holds the promise of greater understanding among nations and the coming of a true brotherhood and sister-hood for all humankind.

"While there will be problems to be faced, crises to be met, there will be a great seeking of peoples as individuals toward understanding," said the Canadian seeress. "May we all call upon Divine Love to open our minds and hearts to others and to bless the friendships in our lives."

China

THE "SALESMAN" BROUGHT WITH HIM A BODYGUARD OF ANGELS

Michael Chang had converted to Christianity and had been baptized by a Lutheran missionary in 1936. He had chosen his Christian name after the Archangel Michael, and he had become such an enthusiastic convert that he had opened a store in Tsingkiangpu, Kiangsu Province, that featured Bibles, religious books, hymnals, and other inspirational items.

In 1942 the Imperial Japanese Army had won their war against China; among their objectives was the removal and confiscation of all Christian materials. Chang knew that it was only a matter of time before his shop was stripped of its inventory. Most of the shop owners of his acquaintance had already been visited by Japanese marines who loaded all Christian-oriented items onto a truck. One of the shopkeepers, who had protested the act, had been severely beaten.

And then came the day that Chang had dreaded. It was early afternoon when a Japanese truck with five marines stopped in front of his shop. The truck was already half-filled with Christian books, Bibles, and religious tracts. The marines jumped off the truck and began to walk toward the front door.

But just as they approached the entrance, a well-dressed Chinese man stepped directly in their path and entered the shop ahead of them. Strangely enough, the five marines stopped just outside the door.

Nervously, Chang anticipated the onslaught of the Japanese marines, but he noticed that they had mysteriously halted their invasion of his shop. Incredibly, they seemed to be waiting for the Chinese gentleman to leave.

Chang directed his attention to the man who had entered his establishment. With the war over and China defeated, he could not imagine any Chinese, rich or poor, who would be respected by any member of the Japanese forces of occupation.

"M-may I help you, sir?" Chang did not recognize the

man, though he did know by name nearly every customer who had ever patronized his shop. This man was a total stranger.

The man smiled at him kindly. "I would like to look at the Christian tracts that you have. Have you any on prayer?"

Chang nodded, leading the customer toward a bookshelf in the corner. "Yes, there are a number of tracts on the subject. And I have some excellent books on prayer, as well."

The man took his time browsing through the various books and tracts.

Chang kept one eye on the soldiers at the door, the other on his customer. The man was dressed in a very expensive suit of finest quality. Money would certainly not appear to be a factor in his taking his time to study the printed materials.

When Chang managed a furtive glance at his watch, he was astonished to see that the stranger had been in his shop for nearly two hours.

And still the Japanese marines had not entered to confiscate the Christian materials. They loitered outside the door; they pressed their noses against the windows to look inside; but they did not enter.

"What do those men want?" the stranger asked.

Chang told him that the Japanese were confiscating all

Christian reading material. They had come to take away all of his stock of Bibles, hymnals, tracts, and other books.

"Then I think it would be wise of us to kneel and pray that they go away," the man said, as if it were a simple task to banish five Japanese marines as it would be to brush away five bothersome insects.

The stranger took Chang's hand in his and they knelt to pray.

When the Japanese marines climbed back into the truck and drove away, the two men had been praying for ninety minutes.

Soon after they heard the sound of the truck driving away, the well-dressed Chinese gentleman got to his feet and indicated that Chang should do likewise.

"What you must do now, Michael," the stranger said, "is to load up as many books and tracts as you can and hide them away before the Japanese return. People will need the comfort and inspiration of these materials during the difficult days ahead."

With those words, the man left Chang's shop.

Before Chang could puzzle through any of the extraordinary events of the afternoon, Benny Lee, a Christian friend, ran into his shop. "Michael, are you all right? Where are all the soldiers? Was there a fight? Was anyone hurt?"

Chang placed a tranquil hand on Benny's shoulder.

"Calm down. I'm fine. The Japanese soldiers left. It was a miracle."

Benny laughed, then quickly sobered. "A miracle of might, my friend. But you must get out of here and take your soldier friends with you before those Japanese marines return with reinforcements."

Chang shook his head in confusion. "What 'soldier friends' are you talking about, Benny?"

"Why, the twelve who protected you all afternoon, of course!"

When Chang finally convinced his friend that he did not know what he was talking about, Benny explained that he had been standing quietly outside near the Japanese truck. He had heard the Japanese marines complaining that they were outnumbered and inadequately armed to enter the store and face the twelve tough-looking Chinese soldiers who stood shoulder-to-shoulder inside. Bands of Chinese guerrilla fighters still resisted the invasion of their homeland, and the Japanese marines were reluctant to face their wrath for the sake of a few Bibles.

"They decided to attempt to wait out the Chinese soldiers, thinking they would soon vacate your shop and leave them to their task of confiscating your inventory," Benny said. "But after nearly four hours of waiting outside, they finally gave up. But you know they'll return soon with more men."

Chang told his friend that there had been no Chinese guerrilla fighters in his store. "The stranger who prayed with me must have been an angel with heavenly powers from God who made those marines think that they saw my shop full of angry soldiers."

Chang remembered the angelic visitor's parting admonition to secret away as many inspirational materials as possible for the days of trial ahead. He agreed with Benny that the Japanese would soon come back with reinforcements, and he asked him to help him carry off as many books and tracts as possible before they returned.

Michael Chang often told the story of his angelic visitor during the years of Japanese occupation, and his remarkable account gave many men and women the inspiration they needed to survive the time of tribulation.

Denmark

The Angel Boarded the Train with Sad News

Rolfe Ludvigsen, one of our correspondents from Denmark, provided us with an account of an angel that appeared to his mother and him on board a train when he was a small boy.

"It was in the winter of 1953," Rolfe said. "My maternal grandmother had developed cancer, and I was accompanying my mother on a journey to visit her. Grandmother Larsen lived in a small village near the German border, and since we lived up north in Frederikshavn, it was quite a long train ride in those days."

Although he was only a child, Rolfe knew that his mother was very concerned about Grandmother Larsen. "I had heard her discussing the situation with my father before we left home. She was afraid that the cancer had spread, and she wanted to bring Grandmother back with us to receive better medical attention in a larger city."

To make matters even worse on the trip, Rolfe could tell that his mother was very uncomfortable on the train. "I knew that she had to be exhausted, but she seemed unable to relax or to fall asleep."

The two of them had been sitting quietly when they saw a woman dressed in white enter the door at the end of their coach.

"I remember well her features," Rolfe said. "She was extremely beautiful, with unusually large blue eyes. Dressed completely in white, she seemed almost to be shining. She seemed quite tall, and I knew that she was looking directly at my mother and me."

Rolfe recalled feeling uneasy and asking his mother about the lady who had just entered their coach: "Do you know her, Mother? She seems to be staring at us."

Before his mother could answer, the woman walked up the aisle and took the seat opposite them. She smiled warmly, and then spoke directly to his mother, addressing her by her first name. "I have a message for you, Klara," she said.

Rolfe remembered his mother frowning in puzzlement

and shifting in her seat. "Do I know you?" she asked the stranger. "Have we ever met?"

The woman nodded to Rolfe's mother, and then said, "I have always known you, Klara." Then the beautiful stranger placed her palms over his mother's trembling hands and said, "I will soon come for your mother, dear. I will take her home with me."

Rolfe recalled how his mother began to weep and shake her head in protest. "Who . . . who are you? Why do you say such things to me?"

The tall woman smiled down at them as she rose to leave. "You know who I am. I'll not see you again until the day when I come to take you home, dear Klara."

With those words, Rolfe said, the lovely, statuesque woman turned, walked to the end of the coach, and stepped out of the door.

Rolfe tried his best to comfort his weeping mother by putting his little arms around her neck and hugging her.

"What has so upset your mother, boy?" asked the woman in the seat behind them. "Is she ill?"

"The lady in white said some things that made her cry," Rolfe replied.

"What lady in white?" the woman wanted to know. "There's no such woman in this coach."

Rolfe tried his best to explain. "She's not seated in this coach, but she came in and sat opposite us for a while. She just left . . . only minutes ago. You must have seen her."

The woman scowled and shook her head. "I'm directly behind you, boy. I saw no woman dressed in white sitting with you for even a second. There's been no such lady in this coach."

By now, other passengers had joined in the conversation. Everyone firmly denied having seen a beautiful woman in white enter the coach and sit opposite Mrs. Ludvigsen and her son. Rolfe said that he will never forget his childish anger and frustration with the men and women as, one by one, they all refuted his account of the strange lady.

On the brink of tears, he asked his mother for confirmation and support. After all, it was *she* who had been brought to tears by their mysterious visitor. "She *was* here, wasn't she, Mommy?"

"She answered me in a soft whisper that I will hear in my mind all the rest of my life," Rolfe said. " 'She was the Angel of Death, my dear son. She was kind enough to prepare me for the death of Grandmother Larsen. Pray that you do not see that particular angel again for many, many years.' "

According to Rolfe, his grandmother passed away three days after they had arrived. "I know that Mother was much better able to bear the emotional pain because of the forewarning that she had received from the beautiful angel on the train. Mother is nearly eighty. Although she knows a return visit from the lovely woman in white is inevitable, she has told me that she is in no hurry to meet her again."

Egypt

*H*IS GUARDIAN'S GUIDING LIGHT PROTECTS HIM

It is from the ancient Egyptians and Mesopotamians that we gain our first real insights into the human mind and its search for spiritual truths. These ancient peoples recognized a hierarchy of supernatural beings that ruled over various parts of the universe, Earth, and the lives of human beings. They also believed in lower levels of entities that might be either benevolent or hostile in their actions toward humans.

The ancient Mesopotamians called their spiritual guardians *shedu* and *lamassu*. The *lamassu* were often depicted as lions or bulls with humanlike heads and large wings, and their representations were placed at the entrances of temples to ward off evil.

The commonfolk considered these guardian spirits to be very accessible, and an ancient invocation, or prayer, asks that the good *shedu* walk on one's right hand and the good *lamassu* walk on one's left.

The ancient Egyptians believed that the *ka* was an invisible spirit double that was born with each individual and accompanied him or her on the pathway of Earth life as a guardian or protector.

As we observe throughout this text, all cultures have a tradition of a guardian spirit for each individual human soul. In the early 1980s, during a trip to Egypt, Brad Steiger made the acquaintance of Abdel, a Cairo attorney, who told him that he knew that the spirit of an old street peddler was his guardian angel. We'll retell Abdel's story here, because it is an interesting one—and it indicates the presence of an unseen protector.

WHEN HE WAS just a boy of four or five, Abdel was fascinated by an elderly street peddler's cigarette lighter. The old man had bartered for an American soldier's Zippo lighter during World War II, and he bragged that the lighter would never fail him. He would even bet with street gamblers that it would be able to light so many times in a row. The peddler became so identified with the battered old Zippo lighter that people in the streets started calling him "Torchbearer."

Abdel's father had taught him that it was a blessing to be kind to the poor, so the boy was always certain to perform some little act of kindness for old Torchbearer—such as bringing him a bit of bread that he had not finished at breakfast.

The peddler died when Abdel was about nine. The old man's friends said that they had buried him with his trusty Zippo lighter.

"Everyone missed seeing old Torchbearer in the streets," Abdel recalled. "He had always been a kind and cheerful man."

One night not long after Torchbearer had passed away, Abdel made the mistake of taking an unfamiliar shortcut home. Suddenly he found himself in an alley that was so dark that he could not see his hand in front of his face.

"I was frightened out of my wits," Abdel said. "What if stray dogs attacked me? What if I wandered all night, becoming more lost by the minute? I was about to burst into tears when I suddenly saw a small ball of flame appear just in front of me. I knew that it was old Torchbearer guiding me to safety. I could even smell the lighter fluid from his old Zippo."

On another occasion, when Abdel was seventeen and walking in a section of Cairo unfamiliar to him, the spirit light suddenly flashed into brilliant illumination above some rotting boards on which he was about to step.

"I knew immediately that Torchbearer was signaling a warning to me. When I cautiously examined the boards, I saw that they covered an old, unused well. If my guardian angel had not flashed the light before my eyes, I would have fallen into the deep well and been killed."

Today, as a man in his mid-fifties, Abdel knows without question that people have guardian spirits that look out for them. "Just last year, as I was about to enter a cave in which I had often taken shade during the afternoon heat, Torchbearer flashed his light before my eyes. Now on the alert, I stepped carefully inside with my walking stick poised in front of me. Poisonous snakes had claimed the place as their abode since I had last visited. Torchbearer had saved my skin once again."

NAPOLEON'S DESTINY WAS DECREED BY AN ANGEL IN CAIRO

Napoleon Bonaparte entered the history books long ago as a renowned military strategist and the emperor of France. The legend of his experience with angels, however, is often forgotten. It is said that according to his own testimony Napoleon was visited by a messenger from Heaven who predicted his downfall if he did not curb his lust for power.

At the beginning of his rise to prominence, the soldier-statesman was characterized by his goals of virtue, truth, and justice. But when he realized the elusiveness of these ideals, Napoleon appeared to become obsessed with a shameless desire to conquer the world. Illustrating that angels recognize no human land boundaries, Napoleon received his first angelic warning in Egypt from an angel who identified himself as a guardian of the French nation. The account of the angel's international journey follows.

In 1798, THE very pyramids of Egypt trembled as Napoleon's troops defeated the ten thousand horsemen of the Muslim chief Mourad Bey. Blood saturated the sand as the French routed the Muslims. It seemed at this point as if all of Egypt—and even all of Africa—lay within the grasp of the diminutive military genius.

Napoleon took over Mourad Bey's palace and claimed the extravagant master bedroom as his own. He commanded that he be left alone to enjoy the splendor in solitude, free at last from the responsibilities of his position and the incessant demands of his officers. That night, he slept soundly until near dawn, when a movement in the room awakened him.

Heavy with sleep, his eyes gradually focused on a tall figure dressed entirely in red. "You, sir, are an intruder," Napoleon said angrily. "I demand that you leave at once."

"Draw not your weapon. It will be useless against me," the intruder said in a sepulchral voice. "I am the Red Man. I am the angel who has appeared before the rulers of France for many centuries."

Napoleon was transfixed as the strange visitor continued.

"You are obsessed with power," the being scowled, "and you think not of your people."

Napoleon protested strenuously. "Everything I do is for the good of my subjects."

The Red Man's hollow laughter echoed in the elegant bedroom. "You are an ambitious man. You wish to play God with the destiny of France and all of humanity.

"I know you better than you know yourself," the mysterious stranger went on. "I walked beside you during your quiet, solitary walks when you were a schoolboy at Brienne. Even then you had the magnificent vision of founding an empire that would eclipse all those previously known. I have walked silently beside you as you marched against the armies of Austria on the plains of Italy. And today when the horsemen of Mourad Bey were crushed beneath your heel, you envisioned yourself as master of an Oriental throne."

"And why not?" Napoleon demanded. "I have conquered Egypt, and even now my ships lie in the harbor of Alexandria."

The angel shook his head. "Your ships are *not* in the harbor of Alexandria. Your order was not obeyed. If your own officers rebel against you, how can you hope to conquer the world?"

"You lie!" Napoleon shouted. "How could you know such things?"

The Red Man's eyes narrowed in impatience. "In less than a year you will return to France having failed to conquer Egypt. The might of England, Russia, and Turkey will be allied against you. France will soon be in a state of chaos."

"Nonsense!" Napoleon sneered. "Should France ever be in trouble, I will return and overthrow the miserable officials responsible for such a disgrace."

The angel turned and began to leave. "I have warned you," he said before he made his exit. "Curb your ambition and heed the threats of your opponents. Control your lust for absolute power before you perish without friends or a country. I leave you now."

As every student of history knows, Napoleon's Egyptian campaign failed. The prophecy of the Red Man, the angelic messenger whose manifestation had been recorded by many French monarchs before Napoleon, was fulfilled precisely as he had warned the feisty Corsican.

ELEVEN YEARS LATER, on a foggy morning in 1809, Napoleon's muddy black boots stomped across the luxurious carpet in an Austrian palace. The French army had decimated the Austrian troops at the brutal battle of Wagram, and now Napoleon prepared to dictate his harsh terms of peace for the defeated nation.

At midnight, as he dozed at a desk covered by maps dotted with colored pins, he was awakened by the Red Man.

In the same deep, hollow voice, the being again identified himself as a messenger from Heaven. "I come to warn you that unless you cease your present campaigns at once, you will be utterly destroyed. You have just four years to accomplish complete peace in Europe. Four years, no more." The angel vanished.

Napoleon told a number of his aides about the mysterious Red Man, then chose to dismiss the incident and continue with the stern realities of his war machine.

THE RED MAN made his third and final appearance to the Emperor Napoleon on January 1, 1814. Napoleon was afflicted with legions of enemies, both in France and in the nations allied against him. Although he had shut himself up with orders that absolutely no one was to disturb him, the angel manifested before him once again. The Red Man told him that it would be all over for him in three months unless he made immediate peace.

"That's impossible," Napoleon complained. "I need more time."

The angel admonished him sternly. "You must negotiate a peace in three months or you will be disgraced."

"A year," Napoleon tried to bargain. "I cannot do as you ask. It is impossible."

"I cannot be swayed by human entreaties," the angel said firmly. "I am but a messenger whose sole mission is to warn you as I am instructed."

"Grant me a year," the Emperor pleaded.

"Three months," the Red Man repeated before vanishing.

THE FOLLOWING WEEKS were disastrous for Napoleon. In an imprudent move, he left Paris unprotected while he took his armies on a campaign to the east. The allied forces moved into the city and captured it. Mobs formed in the streets. The empire crumbled.

Exactly three months after his final conversation with the Red Man, the National Assembly held a secret meeting and demanded Napoleon's abdication.

England

HIS GUARDIAN ANGEL
TWICE SAVED HIS LIFE

Arthur Montgomery of Tunbridge Wells, Kent, saw his guardian angel for the first time when he was a boy of ten during the Battle of Britain in 1940.

"Our family spent nights in a nearby public air raid shelter," Arthur said. "Grandfather Pearson insisted that if he were going to die under Nazi bombs, he wanted to perish in his own house, not trapped with hundreds in a hole in the ground; but Mother always managed to drag him along with us."

Arthur's father was away in the army, but his uncle

Lawrence joined the Air Raid Precautions for night duty, and the boy sometimes managed to talk his way into going along.

"On this particular night, the Nazi bombers seemed to appear out of nowhere," Arthur remembered. "Suddenly the sirens were howling, and within minutes bombs began to fall close at hand. In the confusion, I became separated from Uncle Lawrence."

Uncertain whether to try to make a dash for the public shelter where he knew his mother and grandfather were huddled with hundreds of others, Arthur weighed his options. He could see a sturdy-looking house that he knew was quite deserted but could provide a safe haven. Or there was an old brick toolshed just down the block that would offer room enough for a ten-year-old to be secure.

"I knew that I must decide quickly. Bombs were screaming down within a few hundred yards of me and getting even closer."

Arthur decided on the deserted house and made a run for it.

"But just as I entered the door, I was met by a most imposing figure of a tall, silver-haired man dressed in a white robe. 'Leave this place at once,' he ordered me in a deep, commanding voice. 'It will be bombed in seconds. Run quickly to the toolshed. You will be safe there!' And then, that quickly, he disappeared."

Arthur was barely inside the toolshed when bombs blasted the house into rubble and sent shrapnel and bricks clattering down on roofs and streets.

"Mother was furious with Uncle Lawrence when we were all united later that evening," Arthur said. "I made it quite clear that I was the one to blame, not poor Uncle. And besides, the important thing was that we were all alive—and that I had most certainly met, and been saved by, my guardian angel."

ARTHUR WAS NOT privileged to encounter his guardian angel again until forty years had gone by.

"It was 1980, and I was now fifty years old and running to catch a bus," Arthur said. "It seemed as though I was about to make the stop before it pulled away when I distinctly felt something tugging at my coat and slowing me down. In my peripheral vision I was astonished to see the form of a tall man holding on to my coat."

Fearing that a mugger was attempting to rob him, Arthur spun around, holding his briefcase at chest level.

"I was about to slam the case into my attacker's face when I was startled to behold my silver-haired, white-robed guardian angel. 'It's you!' was all I could manage to say."

Never one to waste or to mince words, the angelic being came right to the point. "If you had kept running after that bus, you would have had a heart attack. Go straight away to your physician. Now!"

Once again, his cosmic benefactor disappeared as quickly as he had materialized. But Arthur was as obedient as he had been when he was a ten-year-old boy surviving the Battle of Britain.

"I figured if the blessed fellow was right then, he was right now," Arthur said. "Although I felt well enough, my physician said that my image of excellent health was an illusion maintained because I had not slowed down enough to listen to my body. According to him, if I had not come in to have my heart and cholesterol and so forth checked when I did, and had not begun a proper medical regimen, Mother Nature would have slowed me down with a heart attack. Once again, my guardian angel had saved my life."

An Angel Sends an Expectant Mother to a Better Doctor

In the mid-1930s, Rev. Maurice Elliott of Lincolnshire published a small book entitled *A Modern Miracle*, in which he related the extraordinary details of the appearance of an angel messenger who manifested to save the lives of his wife and their unborn child. Mrs. Elliott's attending medical physician had assured her that her life and that of her baby would be certain to be snuffed out if she did not submit to the operation that he prescribed.

A specialist, summoned to offer a second opinion, agreed with the Elliotts' doctor that the only chance the expectant mother had of recovery was to undergo the surgery at once—even if "the result would be doubtful."

Reverend Elliott and his wife were extremely nervous about the recommended surgery, and felt a profound lack of confidence in their regular physician's ability to perform the operation safely and successfully. They began to pray earnestly for God's guidance.

That night in their home, a spiritual messenger, a "tall man of fine physique, attired in dazzling white garments," suddenly appeared before Reverend and Mrs. Elliott. The angel told them to travel to the office of a surgeon named Thomas Pearson, who practiced in Brighton, forty miles away. This doctor, the angel promised them, had the necessary skill to perform the required operation without risk to either mother or child.

The couple obediently followed the heavenly being's instructions, with the result that both the mother and her baby were saved.

Reverend Elliott's book included affidavits signed by his wife, by Dr. Pearson, and by an eminent gynecologist—all vouching for the truth of the appearance of the angelic messenger and the success of the subsequent surgery.

In 1936, in his massive work of research entitled *Does Man Survive?*, George Lindsay Johnson included his interview with Reverend Elliott regarding additional details of the above story.

"The angel messenger was a man of very fine physique and above the average height," Reverend Elliott told Johnson. "His age appeared to be about forty years. His eyes, hair, and voice were full of life; in fact, he radiated life. In comparison with him, we are 'existing' rather than 'living.' I cannot describe his presence; it was electric.

"He appeared to us after we had asked God to send us help. He came in answer to our prayers, and he promised to lead us to a surgeon who would take care of 'the little sleeper within.' He told us to go to Brighton and to seek out a surgeon named Dr. Thomas Pearson."

Once the Elliotts had traveled to Brighton, the angel met them there and guided them to a hotel at which the surgeon happened to be staying.

"After Dr. Pearson had finished talking to us," Reverend Elliott told Johnson, "the angel walked with us back to the train station. He wore sandals and seemed to pass through matter, i.e., through the people who passed by close to us on the journey. He was invisible to all but us.

"He finally gave us parting instructions and vanished suddenly, but not without saying good-bye."

Mrs. Elliot confidently returned to Brighton for her surgery on the appointed date, secure in the knowledge that the surgical skills of Dr. Pearson had received the highest of recommendations.

France

HER TRIP TO HEAVEN INSPIRED HER TO RETURN TO PAINTING

In August 1990, while on holiday in Toulon in south-eastern France, thirty-two-year-old Tina Moncrief of Reims took a nasty fall down a steep cliff and suffered a severely fractured skull, a broken leg, and several cracked ribs. The two German hikers who discovered her limp body thought at first that she was dead.

"Once I was brought to the hospital, I slipped in and out of consciousness for two or three days," Tina wrote in her account of her experience. "During those first two days when, indeed, I was just barely clinging to life, I was given a magnificent glimpse of paradise by my guardian angel.

"Immediately after the fall, I felt my spirit, my true consciousness, leaving my body. I seemed at first to be spinning, then rising higher and higher until I could view my crumpled body on the rocks below."

Tina assumed that she had been killed and that her soul was leaving her body. "I saw what appeared to be a very long, dark tunnel. I seemed to be drawn toward it, and I felt a brief moment of fear as I supposed that I was entering the final darkness of death and the loss of all consciousness."

But then Tina saw a door in the tunnel with bright light coming from it. As she drew nearer, she could hear the distinct sounds of choral music floating toward her.

"I felt very comforted and no longer afraid. And then I saw my guardian angel. Although the angelic being was tall, commanding, and glowing with a soft illumination, I somehow recognized it by its energy as the elderly woman who had suddenly appeared to pull me out of the path of a speeding automobile when I was seven."

Tina said that she could not determine the gender of her angel guardian. "Even its voice was somehow devoid of any distinctive male or female intonation, but the words that the being spoke to me were very calming, very inspirational. I felt so much love emanating from this wonderful, compassionate angel."

As Tina glanced at the heavenly environment around them, she saw lovely green meadows, stately trees, numerous angelic beings, and a wide variety of animals. "My section of paradise looked very much like a super-enriched Earth. The colors seemed brighter and richer. Everything seemed to be stepped-up in intensity."

After she felt she had been living in Heaven for at least a week, her guardian angel surprised her by saying that she was only visiting paradise for a short while.

"It is not yet your time, my child," the lovely entity said. "We've only brought you here for a few Earth hours so that you can be 'out of the way,' so to speak, while the doctors work on your body and your physical self begins to restore itself."

Tina felt a rush of disappointment. She liked it there. And her life in Reims as a secretary really hadn't been going anywhere special.

"You've needed this time to slow your pace," the angel told her. "You came into this world with a great talent for painting. You gave up your art to follow business pursuits which really haven't worked out all that well for you."

Tina acknowledged the truth of the angel's assessment of her life to the present time.

"Now, my dear," her guardian angel smiled, "while you are recuperating from your injuries, you will have plenty of time to resume painting."

Once again everything went black.

"When I opened my eyes, a nurse was calling my name," Tina remembered. "My consciousness returned to pain, but in spite of my injuries and my discomfort, I was filled with a renewed enthusiasm for life."

As soon as she was able to sit up, Tina gave a nurse money to buy her some colored pencils and a sketch pad. By the time she was released from the hospital, she was ready to begin transforming blank canvas into brilliant portraits of heavenly beings with her paintbrushes.

"At present," she concluded, "I am forced by my financial condition to be an after-work and weekend painter. However, I know within my heart that I will soon be able to paint portraits of angels and heavenly scenes as my lifework."

ANGELS OF LOURDES PERFORMED A MIRACLE FOR THE DOCTOR

At a hospital not far from the healing shrine at Lourdes, Dr. Alexis Carrel and his French colleague, a well-known surgeon from Bordeaux, carefully examined a patient whose entire immediate family had died of tuberculosis.

The patient herself, Marie Bailey, had tubercular sores, lesions in her lungs, and peritonitis. Although she might have died at any moment, a group of her relatives had made it possible for her to travel to Lourdes so that she might pray for healing. She believed that her guardian angel and the Blessed Mother had promised her a cure.

As a matter of scientific curiosity, Dr. Carrel had asked to be allowed to examine a number of patients before they visited the shrine. Marie Bailey was one of those who had consented to such an examination, since Dr. Carrel was one of the foremost medical authorities in the world. A French-born American surgeon and an experimental biologist, he had won the Nobel Prize in physiology or medicine in 1912 for his extensive work in suturing blood vessels and transplanting organs.

Marie's white face looked emaciated, and her abdomen was swollen into a misshapen lump. Her ears and nails were already turning a vivid blue. Her pulse raced at an incredible 150 beats per minute.

"I have faith, doctor," Marie answered in response to Carrel's inquiry as to why she had wished to visit the healing shrine in spite of her great physical pain. "My angel has told me that the Blessed Mother shall heal me because of my faith."

After he left the patient, Carrel shook his head sadly and whispered, "She's doomed. The poor woman is on the very brink of death. No act of the angels or mental suggestion of divine healing can save her. She's too far gone."

At that point in his life, any religious concepts that Carrel might have held when he was younger and more idealistic had been destroyed by his various scientific investigations. He had come to Lourdes as a skeptic among the pilgrims to study the claims of alleged cures, but he doubted that he would see any authentic healings.

The only thing that would convince him, he had told his medical colleagues, was the cure of an organic disease, such as the disappearance of a cancer, the regrowth of a bone, or the complete correction of a congenital abnormality.

By the time Carrel and his colleagues arrived at the shrine, a good number of the patients had already approached the spring where the simple village girl Bernadette had seen the Beautiful Lady in 1858. Marie Bailey had been carried to the front of the shrine. Somehow she had managed to get to her feet and stand.

Dr. Carrel was startled when Marie suddenly stiffened as if a powerful force had surged through her pain-wracked body. The woman's stretcher bearers stared uncomprehendingly at her.

Marie's face clouded. Then, a few moments later, as if she had discarded a somber mask of pain, her paleness lifted and was immediately replaced by a healthy, rosy hue.

Before the assembled doctors' very eyes, Marie's grotesquely swollen abdomen was flattened. The nervousness left her body as her pulse rate calmed. Her respiration appeared to be normal.

"The angels and the Blessed Mother have healed me," Marie said. Then she added, in a soft voice, "I would really like a glass of milk."

A bit later, when her request was fulfilled, doctors noted that it was the first nourishment that she had been able to consume in almost a week.

After he had witnessed the amazing act of healing, Carrel did not trust himself to conduct an objective re-examination of Marie Bailey. When the group returned to the hospital, the scientist insisted that three additional physicians assist in the examination.

"We can only verify what you already know," one of them stated after giving the patient a thorough physical evaluation. "Marie Bailey has been cured."

Orthodox medical science can offer no easy explanation for what Dr. Carrel and the other physicians witnessed. Only an hour before, Marie Bailey had been dying. She had suffered for years from tuberculosis, unquestionably an organic disease. Yet she had returned to the hospital a completely cured person. The murky stench of death no longer hung over her. She seemed to have come alive again after the long illness, and her body surged with health and vitality.

Carrel had received from the angels all those elements that he insisted must be present in order to convince him of the reality of a miracle cure.

Just as Marie Bailey had left her illness at Lourdes, so would Dr. Alexis Carrel leave his skepticism in the water of its healing spring. The well-respected scientist remained a devout believer in miraculous healings until his death in 1944.

NOSTRADAMUS AND THE PROPHECIES OF THE ANGEL ANAEL

Although the prophet Nostradamus has become very well known, few people are aware that the mystic received his world-famous prophecies from an angel. Interestingly, even the most detailed and distinguished of the documentaries depicting Nostradamus's life neglect to mention the source of his futuristic inspirations.

ON DECEMBER 14, 1503, in Saint-Rémy in Provence, Michel de Nostredame began a life that was destined to be filled with political intrigue, Renaissance rationalism, and prophetic writings. Sometime before his birth, his Jewish parents decided to become Catholics because of a papal edict decreeing disfavor to all who were not Christians. By the time Michel was a young man, the religious practice of the family had become a curious mixture of Catholic and Jewish customs and belief constructs, blended with a generous dose of mysticism.

When he was old enough, Nostradamus was sent off to study liberal arts at Avignon. Although he was most interested in studying the stars, his practical-minded father insisted that he become a man of medicine.

After four years of intensive study in Parisian medical schools, Nostradamus passed his examination and was allowed to establish a practice. His practice was disrupted when the Black Death struck Southern France.

The young doctor was considered very successful in his treatment of the plague, and he gained a reputation as a great healer. Later, he returned to academia, earned his doctorate, and accepted a position at the university. His unquenchable desire to travel and to seek out esoteric wisdom made him unhappy in a university setting, but by now he had a wife and two children, and his deep affection for his family enabled him to achieve some level of contentment.

When another outbreak of the plague took his wife and children, Nostradamus was grief-stricken. He who had saved so many lives from the Black Death had been unable to keep his own family safe from its deadly embrace. He abandoned his medical practice and set about wandering across Europe.

It was during this period that he discovered that the angel Anael was guiding him and blessing him with prophetic powers.

As he wandered from city to city, Nostradamus began to make predictions that made him famous. While in Italy, he saw a young Francisan monk approaching his party. Although his companions commented that the young cleric was but an ex-swineherd named Felice Peretti, the prophet bent one knee to the ground as he passed. Afterward, when questioned about his strange behavior, Nostradamus answered solemnly that he must submit himself and bend a knee before His Holiness. The puzzling reply was not made clear to Nostradamus's friends until 1585, when Cardinal Peretti became Pope Sixtus V.

NOSTRADAMUS BEGAN TO write almost exclusively in poetic quatrains not long after he was brought to the court of France by Catherine de' Medici, the Queen Mother. She was concerned for her children and she demanded that the prophet disclose their future.

We can imagine the angel Anael whispering in his ear

that he must proceed with caution on such dangerous ground. In a prophetic flash from the angel, Nostradamus was shown that all the children were destined to die young as the result of political intrigues.

Nostradamus quietly absorbed the inner vision that Anael disclosed. He stood before the Queen Mother, searching for some appropriate manner in which to express such tragedy. It would be sheer folly to predict to the ruthless Catherine de' Medici that her progeny were destined for miserable deaths.

And then, with Anael's guidance, the words came—all of them accurate, but couched in obscure poetic language.

The Queen Mother seemed satisfied to be left to interpret the mystical verses, and Nostradamus left the palace with his head still attached to his neck. He had received Anael's inspiration to begin to cloak ugly truths in poetic utterance—and thus preserve his own skin.

Honduras

An angel sent his soul back to his body

Honduran Gilbert Lopez told us of the time that he became very ill when he was living in the coastal city of La Ceiba.

"Although my body seemed incapable of movement, my senses essentially remained alert and aware," he said. "My wife Guadalupe and my best friend, Dr. Claudio Cardoza, kept a faithful vigil at my bedside. From time to time other friends would stop by to visit only briefly, and I watched their grim faces as they beheld my desperate condition."

At the point when Dr. Cardoza was nearly exhausted from maintaining a regular physician's schedule as well as spending long hours at Gilbert's bedside, a cheery Catholic nurse from the United States volunteered to help keep watch.

"Sister Veronica's arrival could not have been better timed," Gilbert said. "I was beginning to worry more about my friend Claudio's collapsing from fatigue than I was about my own condition."

Gilbert remembered that he was quite aware that he might die. "But I was not afraid. I was simply astonished that I was lying there so helplessly on my bed. The illness had come on so quickly that I had not had time mentally to prepare myself for the possibilities of death or a long period of convalescence."

One night, as his condition was worsening, Gilbert heard Sister Veronica telling Guadalupe that he must have a transfusion of plasma. "She went on to say that she knew of only one bottle of that precious fluid available in the entire town."

Several hours later, Dr. Cardoza and Sister Veronica were able to give Gilbert the needed transfusion—but then he went into shock. "I have dim memories of shivering violently. It seemed as though the slightest movement brought undue stress on my heart. *And then my heart stopped completely!*"

At that moment, Gilbert became aware that there

seemed to be two versions of himself present in the room. There was the pale, sweat-drenched, slack-jawed creature lying on the bed. And there was the Real Gilbert standing off to the side, somehow aware of everyone's thoughts and feelings.

"My wife was crying. Claudio sighed deeply and tears came to his eyes. 'We've lost him,' he said softly."

Sister Veronica was still bending over Gilbert's body. "No, he will come back. I do not think that it is his time to die. I do not think God will take him at this time."

Sister Veronica's faith appeared to be stronger than her medical knowledge. "I wanted to tell her that it was all right. I was at peace. But then I became aware of a beautiful angel in a long, flowing robe standing at my right side. I could not tell the sex of the entity, and even its voice seemed genderless. Waves of rainbow-hued light emanated from a brilliantly illuminated arc around its head. I assumed that I had died and was being met by my guardian angel, but the entity smiled at me and said, 'Your Earth time is not yet completed. You have much more work to do. You must return to your body.' "

A part of Gilbert's consciousness watched Dr. Cardoza injecting something into his arm. "I learned later that the injection was his last, desperate attempt to start my heart beating again. Frantically, Sister Veronica began searching for a pulse. 'I've got one!' she shouted in triumph."

Gilbert said that it was as if he were returning to his

body from the very farthest reaches of the universe. "It took me quite a while to return to full consciousness, but I knew that I would not die. My guardian angel stayed with me until I spoke my first words, asking if I might have a sip of water."

Guadalupe clutched his hand, her face wet with tears. "We were so afraid that we had lost you!"

Claudio grasped his other hand. "You came back to us, my dear friend!"

In a hoarse whisper, Gilbert agreed. "My guardian angel heeded Sister Veronica's diagnosis. It was not yet time for me to return home to Heaven."

Hungary

ANGELS SENT A VISION OF AN ASSASSINATION THAT CHANGED THE COURSE OF WORLD HISTORY

Many scholars of religious experience believe that one of the most amazing prophetic dreams in our century was sent by the angels on June 28, 1914, to Dr. Josef von Lanyi, a Roman Catholic bishop in Hungary. The dream proved to be of great political, as well as spiritual, significance; it was the start of a series of major events that changed the course of world history.

In the dream, the Bishop viewed himself reading his morning mail. As he did so, his attention was directed to a large envelope with an ominous black border. Strangely enough, he recognized the handwriting on the envelope to be the forceful script of Archduke Franz Ferdinand, heir apparent to the Austro-Hungarian Empire. Bishop Lanyi was quite certain of the handwriting because the Archduke had been his pupil many years before.

Inside the envelope was a photograph of a crowded street scene. Soldiers lined the road to keep a crowd from the pathway of a luxurious automobile carrying the Archduke, his wife Sophie, an Austrian general, and another army officer.

Suddenly the photograph seemed to come to life, and two men, quite young, rushed from behind the guards and fired revolvers at the Archduke and his wife.

In his dream, the startled Bishop dropped the photograph, then noticed that the Archduke had written a message on its back: "I wish you to know that my wife and I will perish this very day as a result of political assassination. Dear Bishop Lanyi, please say godly prayers and holy Masses for us, and I beseech you to remain devoted to our poor orphaned children."

The letter was dated Sarajevo, June 28, 1914, 3:30 A.M.

The Bishop awakened, disturbed by such a terrible dream. He looked at the clock. It was exactly 3:30 A.M.

Immediately the clergyman went to his desk and wrote down every last detail of the unsettling dream.

After completing this task, he began to say his rosary fervently.

When his butler entered Lanyi's room at 5:30 A.M., he anxiously inquired if the Bishop were ill. Bishop Lanyi told the man that he was extremely upset by a terrible dream in which the holy angels had shown him an awful event that would befall Archduke Franz and Duchess Sophie. He ordered the butler to gather the entire household so that he might say a Mass for the souls of the beloved royal couple.

Bishop Lanyi was a very thorough individual. After the Mass in the chapel had been completed, he told those assembled of his vision and asked that they sign the notes and sketches which he had drawn up from his memory of the dream.

Although there is no record that Bishop Lanyi made any attempt to warn the Crown Prince and his wife of the impending assassination, it is known that the churchman did spend the rest of that day in the chapel, praying continuously for the souls of his country's royalty.

At the same time, several hundred miles away, Archduke Franz Ferdinand and Duchess Sophie were preparing for a day of festivities which would be inaugurated by a lavish parade. Cheering crowds lined the streets of Sarajevo, capital of the province of Bosnia, and the very sight of such warmth and frivolity made the Archduke scoff at the warning that he had received that someone might attempt to assassinate him.

Still, Franz Ferdinand was a Hapsburg and a realist. He

was quite aware that if someone among the subjected Serbs did truly seek his life, today's celebration of Vidovdan, their national holiday, would be the perfect time to kill him.

Just before the Crown Prince entered the waiting automobile, he turned to one of his officers and remarked, "It would not surprise me if we were to receive a few bullets today."

The prospect of sudden death did not frighten Franz Ferdinand. He had been instructed from early childhood that he might be required to make his peace with God at the most unexpected moment. The Hapsburg susceptibility to a sudden embrace from the Angel of Death was intensified in Franz Ferdinand's tubercular youth, during which he felt he was living on borrowed time.

The automobile carrying the royal couple did not travel far before it approached the spot where two conspirators stood waiting with hidden revolvers.

The first assassin was nervous and unsteady, for even at point-blank range he missed both of his startled targets.

The second malefactor, the Serbian nationalist Gavrilo Princip, was much steadier and more accurate. His bullets struck first the Archduke, then the Duchess, killing them instantly.

At 3:30 P.M. Bishop Lanyi was interrupted at his prayers to be informed of the deaths of his beloved former pupil Franz Ferdinand and his wife.

———

SO OFTEN WE have seen that the great events of history appear to cast their shadows before them, and so often the angels seem to have had the knowledge to forewarn but not to change the cosmic throw of the dice. The blood of the royal house of Hapsburg had spilled forth from Bishop Lanyi's precognitive dream to become a disastrous reality—and the crimson pool of blood seeping from the violated bodies of Franz Ferdinand and Sophie would flow in ever-widening circles.

On July 28, a month to the day after the Serb Princip had murdered their Crown Prince, Austria declared war on Serbia. Within another week, Germany had declared war on Russia and France, and had invaded Belgium. During that same week, Great Britain declared war on Germany. What the angels had actually shown Bishop Lanyi in that awful vision of assassination was the precipitating event that set the terrible carnage of World War I in motion.

India

THE HOLY REALMS OF ANGELS

Sherry's dear friend Dr. I. C. Sharma was born and educated in India, but came to the United States for further study and research. He taught at the university level in America and was on the advisory board of The Butterfly Center for Transformation, founded by Sherry in the 1970s.

In addition to pursuing his conventional education, Dr. Sharma studied for many years in India under a holy man, His Holiness Param Sant Param Dayal Faqir Chand Ji

Maharaj. Dr. Sharma witnessed firsthand the "uncanny powers" that were attributed to his guru.

"I saw for myself countless miracles and healings, many that seemed completely impossible to explain, that Faqir Ji Maharaj had performed," Dr. Sharma told us. "It wasn't hard to see why he had a following in India of millions and millions."

DR. SHARMA SHARED with Sherry some of his experiences with his guru and the angels and of the realms of the angels. He said the Faqir had the ability to close his eyes and "see" things.

Sometimes he would see angelic beings, but most often he would see a circle of light that would become very bright, like an "inner sun." He would also describe going through a tunnel and coming out on the other side to a "second sky."

Dr. Sharma described what his guru had taught him about this second sky, this place where the angels dwell: "The Light of this region puts to shame the light of a thousand suns and a thousand moons. There is heard a Divine Sound—the sound of Om. There is also the sweet sound of thunder of the clouds that goes on all the time."

He continued, telling that there was yet another realm beyond that, through a "third curtain." "Through the third curtain where one begins to get the news of the spiritual world, this region is called the SUNN. The Faqirs have called it Alam-i-Lahoot. In that place the Souls that abide there bathe in pure bliss. Many people see them as angelic souls," he said.

Attempting to describe these other realms with words is nearly impossible, as they have to be experienced to be comprehended, Sharma confided. "It is as though the Light therein is such that it appears to be a dozen times as brilliant as that in the second sky, or the Trikuti Triangle, as the Faqirs call it.

"In this place there is a 'Tank of Nector' or 'Tank of Immortality'—also called the Mansarovar Lake," Sharma continued. Sharma told us that such tanks and lakes are everywhere, as well as many gardens in full blossom. He evoked these scenes and described them so vividly we could almost smell the heavenly fragrance and feel the purity of a mist bathing and renewing our every cell.

Sharma told us that the Faqir continued to describe higher and higher levels almost as exactly envisioned and described by the Old Testament prophets Ezekiel and Enoch. Sharma, who had also studied the Old and New Testaments of the Bible and the apocrypha, reminded us that Ezekiel and Enoch were taken to these realms of "heavens" by angels, and they described the same "heavenly abodes of angels" as did the Faqir.

✍ DEVA SAVES THE LIVES OF SCHOOLCHILDREN

Rajesh Gupta, a thirty-four-year-old teacher from New Delhi, readily acknowledged the existence of angelic beings.

"To those of us who follow the wisdom teachings of the Hindu tradition, the beings of the good spiritual forces, the mighty, immortal protectors of humankind, are known as *devas*," he explained. "The holy teachings describe them as beings of great mercy and wisdom."

Rajesh went on to tell us that certain of the Hindu traditions recognize that the *devas* may assume many different forms and guises, appearing however it may best suit their goals. In ancient Sanskrit, the name means "a shining being." A *deva*, a dazzling being composed of light, has the power to come to the spiritual seeker as a holy figure, as a lovely winged being, or as one of any number of animals.

"I KNOW THAT it was a *deva* in the form of a large white dog that saved the lives of my students when I was teaching in a remote Indian village in 1988," Rajesh said. "I know many Americans and Europeans think that a poor and hungry nation such as India would not honor the keeping of pets, but Hindus and Buddhists revere all life forms. Dogs are kept by many families, who share whatever food they have with their four-legged friend."

Rajesh remembered vividly the large white dog that approached him while he was eating his lunch. "I could tell at once that there was something special about him. There was a strange look in his eye. I gave him a portion of my sandwich, and I spoke to him in a friendly manner. I know now that he was a *deva* testing me to see if I was worthy."

Later that afternoon, as the students were sitting quietly during a study period, the large white dog appeared at the open door of the small schoolhouse and began to bark fiercely.

"The students began to laugh and to chatter among themselves, their studies completely disrupted by the dog's noisy barking," Rajesh said. "Since it was a very hot afternoon and I knew the students were uncomfortable at their desks, I told them, 'I think our friend wants us to take a recess so that you can play with him for a while.' "

All twenty of Rajesh's students greeted his observation with a cheer, and he dismissed them for a thirty-minute recess.

"Just as I ushered the smallest of my pupils out of the door," Rajesh recalled, "a truck carrying petrol swerved out of control and crashed into the rear of the building. There was a violent explosion, and a searing ball of flame engulfed nearly the entire area where the students only moments before had sat quietly over their textbooks. Two or three students and I, myself, received burns that required some medical treatment, but all of us were alive."

Later, when Rajesh inquired about the large white dog that had saved their lives, none of the children could remember seeing it after they had exited the schoolhouse.

"The little brother of one of my pupils, who lived very near the school, was playing in their front yard when the children ran out of the building after the white dog," Rajesh said. "Although the boy was only three or four years old, he said that he saw not a dog leading the children out of the school, but a beautiful, shining lady in dazzling white robes. I believed him."

Ireland

An angel provided money for the overdue bill

Sixty years ago, Michael Doyle was born near Ballinasloe, Ireland. He has never forgotten the time that an angel brought his mother the money to pay an overdue bill.

"From her birth, my baby sister Kathleen suffered a chronic illness which the doctors said she would one day outgrow—if we could keep her alive," Michael told us. "You see, her bronchial tubes would spasm in such a way that the poor child could inhale but she couldn't exhale unless someone gave her artificial respiration."

Little Kathleen was in and out of hospitals and clinics,

and when she was home the doctor had to visit no less than three times a week.

"I think we were lucky just to scrape by," Michael said. "Although Da made a fairly good living for us, the hospital and doctor bills nearly ate us up. Mother couldn't go back to work, because Kathleen needed constant looking after."

It was in the winter of 1943 that his mother received the money from the angel.

"I was about seven and Kathleen was three or so, and Mother had ordered heavy woolen snowsuits for us to keep away the cold winter winds," Michael continued. "Mother thought that she might be able to squeeze out the money to pay for them by the end of the month of November, but now here it was the middle of March and the bill was long overdue. She knew that if she didn't manage to pay the bill very soon, Da's wages might be garnisheed."

The bill was only a few Irish pounds, around twenty dollars. But, Michael reminded us, in those difficult days of strict rationing in the midst of the strife and stress of World War II, it was a lot of money for a working-class Irish family to set aside for something "extra" like new snowsuits for the kids. He kept expecting his father to grouse about how he and Kathleen could have made do for another winter, but the good man held his peace about the matter.

"I know that mother made a novena to the Blessed

Virgin, praying that somehow she would be able to get enough money to pay the bill," Michael said.

And then their little miracle occurred.

Mrs. Doyle kept a fern on a stand near the front door, and Michael remembered the day that it suddenly began to shed its leaflets.

"It's looking disgraceful, it is," she worried aloud to Michael. "Help me move it back away from the front door. When the weather is warmer, I'll plant it in the yard for the summer."

Michael recalled that his mother lifted the plant, and he flexed his seven-year-old muscles to manhandle the stand.

"As I did so, the doily that had been under the plant slipped off the stand and an envelope that had been under the doily fell to the floor," Michael remembered. "Strangely enough, it was an airmail envelope, and when Mother opened it, she pulled out crisp, new Irish pound notes— enough to pay her bill at the store and maybe just a wee bit extra."

Michael said that his mother was firmly convinced that the Blessed Virgin had heard her prayers and had sent an angel to deliver the desperately needed money. It was certain that neither of his parents had put the money under the fern for safekeeping and then forgotten about it. Money was far too scarce in the Doyle household to misplace a single cent, to say nothing of squirreling any of it away.

And they didn't know anyone who could have sent them an airmail letter. Besides, the envelope was un-addressed.

Da and Michael agreed with Mother. The money had come from the angels.

"I always thought the airmail envelope was a very nice touch," Michael said. "After all, the money had come to us through the air from on high."

Italy

ANGELO'S GUARDIAN ANGEL
SAVED HIM FROM DROWNING

Angelo Diotto of Padua, Italy, has a clear memory of the remarkable event that occurred when he nearly drowned in a swimming pool at the age of ten. He has never forgotten that he was rescued by a heavenly being that identified itself as "Angelo's guardian angel."

Today, as a thirty-eight-year-old adult, Diotto readily admits that he was not a pious little boy. He avoided going to church whenever possible, and his parents grew weary with his constant acts of mischief. The fact that Angelo often behaved like a little devil seemed to make it all the more miraculous that an angel would appear to save him.

The act of angelic intercession took place on July 10, 1968. Angelo had been warned to stay away from the deep end of the swimming pool, but his devil-may-care attitude convinced him that there was nothing to fear if he should decide to jump in. The fact that he didn't yet know how to swim seemed of little consequence.

Angelo decided to jump into the pool at the deep end— and he nearly drowned.

Later, as lifeguards were bringing him around, Angelo said that he had heard beautiful music under the water, and that when he felt the hands of the lifeguards, he did not want them to pull him to the surface.

In fact, after his first few moments of panic, he did not wish to be saved at all.

"I saw things that I had never seen before," Angelo Diotto said. "They were wonderful, beautiful.

"There was a man there who spoke to me and said that he was my guardian angel and that he was always watching over me. He also explained that I often made his task difficult, because I was so mischievous.

"I wanted to run to my guardian angel, but he held both hands up and told me to stay where I was. He said that I should not get too close to him because I was not yet ready to stay where he was. He said that it was unwise, even dangerous, for me to be too near to him, because I must return to the land of the living.

"Then he started to fade away. Everything became a blur, and all of a sudden I was lying on the ground and my mother was crying and men kept pushing some kind of cone over my face."

Ever since that near-death experience as a child, Angelo Diotto said that he took great comfort in knowing that there was an entity who called himself "Angelo's guardian angel," who watched over him wherever he went and whatever he did—even though he is no longer quite so mischievous.

Japan

HE VISITED HIS GRANDFATHER IN ANOTHER DIMENSION

In the spring of 1985, Hiroshi Yashiki of Osaka was one of thousands of young motorbike enthusiasts who spent as many after-school and weekend hours as possible exploring out-of-the way trails in the area.

"I was riding at top speed on a mountain trail when I felt myself going into a slide," Hiroshi stated in his account. "It was near a Shinto shrine, and I knew that I must not strike the holy place with my bike. My family proudly follows the Shinto way, which we revere as the indigenous religion of Japan."

Hiroshi remembered striking an outcropping of rock and spinning like a child's top out of control. "And then this elderly gentleman seemed to reach out and slow me down."

Hiroshi was certain that he must be dead, and the old man was an angel of death. "We believe that there are benevolent *kami* spirits looking out for us, just as you believe that angels guide your life on Earth. I suppose the angels and the *kami* are really one and the same, for all practical purposes. We also venerate our ancestors and believe their spirits remain active participants in our Earth lives."

The elderly man smiled at Hiroshi and squeezed his arm in an affectionate way. "I am not a death *kami*," he said. "You will not meet any of those for a while. Come and sit with me. I will make us some tea."

Hiroshi's genial host indicated a small, neat house near a little mountain stream.

"I kept thinking that there was something familiar about the old man," Hiroshi said. "The thin white mustache, the sparse hair. I had a flash of some old pictures in one of the family albums. Suddenly I knew that he was my grandfather, my mother's father, who died shortly after I was born."

Within the next few moments, the old man was surrounded by elegant beings that glowed with an otherworldly light.

"Aha," the man laughed, moving toward Hiroshi with open arms, "the beloved *kami* have told me that you have guessed who I am. I am your grandfather Kazutoshi!"

Hiroshi received a warm embrace from his grandfather, then asked him if he, too, were now dead.

Grandfather Kazutoshi shook his head. "A nasty blow to the head, that's all. But why must you ride such infernal machines? Their awful noise disturbs all the *kami* who live in the mountain streams and the forest trees."

Hiroshi remembered that the tea his grandfather served him was the most delicious that he had ever tasted.

"It is the only kind that the *kami* drink," the old man explained. "And since they are the very essence of love and generosity, they share their tea and all else with those of us who are in spirit."

Hiroshi wondered where other spirits of the deceased might be.

"They are all around us, my son. They respect our privacy and our time to be alone, so they remain invisible to you."

And why, Hiroshi wanted to know, could he distinguish the benevolent *kami* as only little more than glowing spheres of light?

"You need to learn to see with your spiritual eyes. The loving *kami* are around you always."

Next Hiroshi asked if his grandfather knew how long he would remain in this other world.

"Grandfather told me to look down between my feet. When I did as he bade, I was astonished to see that I could clearly view my physical body all smashed up at the side of the trail, just to the left of the Shinto shrine."

Grandfather Kazutoshi indicated that it would soon be time for Hiroshi to return. "The *kami* will guide you back to your body. Please be more careful, my little one. I do not want our family line to die out because of your recklessness on such noisy mechanical beasts!"

A few minutes later, a man and woman in a car came upon Hiroshi's unconscious body. When the man pulled a flask from his coat pocket and pressed it between Hiroshi's lips, two glowing *kami* entities grabbed the boy on either side and began to swirl around and around with him.

"The next thing I knew, I was back in my body, choking and sputtering on the liquor. After a few minutes, when I was able to sit up, the man and woman were kind enough to take me to a hospital.

"The doctors in attendance diagnosed my injuries as a fractured skull and several bruised ribs. I soon recovered, and I was left with the glorious newfound wisdom of the eternal loved ones who are always near to us as we travel the treacherous pathways of life."

✐N ANGEL OPENS THE TELEPHONE LINE

While we wrote *Angels Around the World*, our youngest daughter, Melissa, was teaching in Japan. Not far from Osaka, she teaches English in Satellite School.

When the giant earthquake hit Japan in 1995, an angel whispered in our ears to turn on the television—there was something we needed to know about immediately! Having learned from experience to trust and obey that voice, we promptly pushed back our chairs, leaving our word processors on as the text cursors flashed away to remind us of the interrupted task at hand.

As soon as the power switch on the television was turned on, it became evident that something of catastrophic proportions had occurred. It took only a few minutes of viewing to find out that an earthquake measuring 7.2 on the Richter scale appeared to have devastated Japan in the Kobe–Osaka region.

Our hearts raced as we ran for the telephone. In dialing the number of Melissa's apartment, it had not even occurred to us to wonder what time it might be in Japan, or when the quake had hit, or whether Melissa would be at home or at the school teaching.

The phone had barely rung when Melissa picked it up, knowing it was us before we spoke. She was okay but extremely shaken—physically and, of course, emotionally. Things had fallen off shelves—dishes, pictures broken, various things in disarray—but thank God the building had not caved in. Nor did it seem that there were buildings down for a couple of blocks or so.

We could talk only long enough to hear she was all right, and the lines went out. We prayed and prayed for her continued protection, as well as for all the people in the area. We did not know at the time we called that the earthquake had occurred many hours before we were finding out about it, and the lines had been down *before* we called.

Somehow, an angel let us reach our daughter and know that she was safe. From that point on, the lines were down for days, and we could only continue to trust that God and His angels would protect our daughter.

THE DEVASTATION WAS so great that it was many weeks, months even, before the actual damage and number of those injured or killed could be known. The view of damage from the air was beyond belief. It looked as if the cities had been hit by bombs rather than by an earthquake. Melissa was just a few miles away from Kobe—the area hardest hit.

Shortly afterward, Melissa and a few friends volunteered to help out in feeding the homeless in the heartbreak of their losses. Although the world reached out to send supplies and aid, that didn't stop the ground from shaking with thousands upon thousands of aftershocks, leaving all to wonder if there would be more of the same on the way. Melissa said that a few of the aftershocks were great enough to take down more buildings, which were already "ajar" from the first thunder.

All one can do in such calamities is hope and pray that angels are watching over as many people as possible, guiding them to safety, or keeping their protective wings over such as Melissa. For all those who didn't make it and for all those who lost loved ones, we extend our compassion and sympathy and trust that angels spirited them to a better place in the heavens above.

Mexico

HER ANGEL HELPED SAVE HER SONS FROM A SINKING CAR

In May 1991, thirty-two-year-old Griselda Dominguez of Zamora, Mexico, was returning home from a brief road-trip with her two sons, nine-year-old Arturo and seven-year-old Alfredo, when her parked automobile somehow slipped out of gear and rolled into a small lake.

"I was nearly hysterical with fear," she said. "My sons were still in the backseat of the car!"

Griselda had been driving for hours. She stopped the car at the side of the road and got out to stretch her legs for a moment or two and to check the map. Arturo and Alfredo were both sound asleep.

"I know that I turned off the ignition and left the car in 'park.' I was ten or twelve yards from the car when I saw that it was moving. The incline to the lake was quite steep, so once it rolled over the edge, it moved very quickly into the water."

As she made a desperate run to catch up with the runaway car, Griselda screamed at her sons to wake up. "I thought that if they woke up in time, they could somehow get free of the car."

To her absolute horror, once the car rolled into the lake, it began to sink.

Griselda shouted a fervent prayer for assistance. There were no other cars on the road. She was alone with her terrible problem. And she was alone with God and the angels.

"Please, Dear Father," she sobbed, "send one of your ministering angels to help me. I cannot lose my sons!"

Griselda plunged into the lake, swimming furiously to catch up to the sinking automobile.

One back window was open . . . open enough to squeeze her sons through.

The boys were now wide awake, screaming their terror. The water covered most of the car's body, but it had not yet reached the open window.

"I fought my way through the water," Griselda recalled. "I knew that I couldn't go on living if my sons died. I was so close, I had to save them."

She felt her blood freeze in her veins when the car settled and water suddenly reached the level of the open window. In another few seconds, the car would be completely underwater.

"I could hear my sons screaming to me to save them. I reached the car just as the water began to rush into the open window and engulf my sons."

And then the miracle occurred.

"If I live to be a hundred, I will never forget what I beheld at that moment," Griselda said. "A beautiful being of glowing light appeared under the car and lifted it up so that the rear window was once again above the waterline. My sons were reaching out for me, and I pulled them free of the sinking car.

"Thank God, my husband and I had invested in swimming lessons for the boys. Arturo, especially, swims like a little fish. Once I had them free of the car, I knew that I would be able to guide them toward the shore."

Griselda had no sooner removed Arturo and Alfredo from the open window when the car slipped completely under the water.

"My guardian angel was gone, but he had held the car above water long enough for me to rescue my sons!"

Alfredo became fatigued as they struggled toward land. But a young couple driving by had seen their plight and quickly parked their own car, and the man plunged in to help Griselda bring her boys to safety.

"I have always been a religious person, and I have also known that I had a guardian angel," Griselda said. "And now I know for certain that his strong hand will be there for me whenever I most need it!"

*H*IS GUARDIAN RESCUED THEM FROM A DARK FORCE THAT INVADED THEIR STRANGE MUTUAL DREAM

On occasion, it seems, a soul bond between a man and a woman can become so strong that they may experience common dreams—or at least an awareness of what the other had been viewing in the dream state. And even in that mysterious in-between universe, our guardian angels will come to our aid and protect us from agents of the Dark Side.

"About ten years ago, in 1985, my wife Aida and I shared a bizarre dream experience that proved to be a most frightening ordeal," Ramon Domenico of Guadalajara, Mexico, told us.

"Truly, my friends," Aida spoke up, "I would have

been carried away by malignant forces if it were not for Ramon."

"And my guardian angel!" Ramon added quickly. "He saved us both."

We urged them to continue with their story.

Aida had retired early that night, and she was fast asleep when Ramon came to bed.

"I doubt if I had been asleep more than a few minutes when I became aware of Aida calling to me for help *in my dream*," Ramon said. "Somehow, I answered her call, and I crossed over *into her dream*!"

Ramon found himself standing in a cave that was dank and surreal, "as if it had been painted by Salvador Dali." Aida stood against a dark, slime-covered wall, cowering before some hideous reptilian creature.

"I was terribly frightened when I first saw the hulking, dragonlike monster slavering over Aida, but then a part of my mind reminded me that this was a dream," Ramon said. "So with a courage to be found only in bottles or in dreams, I charged the monster with my fists swinging."

Ramon told us that it turned out to be a battle royal. "I could feel my fists slamming against the beast's bulk, and his rough, scaly flesh soon made my knuckles bleed. He struck me some fierce blows! Once, I felt his talons rip my cheek, and I cried out in pain as I realized that this was no ordinary dream. Somehow, we seemed to have entered some other reality."

Aida shuddered at the memory. "I felt that we were doomed. It seemed that we were in some world apart from Earth. Ramon was brave, but the awful demon was too strong for him."

"For a while it seemed as though I might be driving the evil thing back," Ramon said, "but then I heard Aida screaming behind me. I looked over my shoulder and saw that the damned monster had called in reinforcements."

Ramon saw that there were now two more demons to keep away from his wife. One brute was holding Aida by the shoulders while another sought to grab her legs so that they might carry her away. Aida was kicking at both of them with all of her strength, and during the struggle one of her pajama legs was torn off at the hip.

"Finally, at that terrible moment," Ramon continued, "I called upon my own guardian angel to help us. I don't know why I didn't think of it before. Aida and I had both felt the presence of angels in our lives. We had been convinced from our first meeting that our guardian angels had brought us together to be man and wife. So I had no doubt that my mental summons, my fervent prayers, would bring us divine assistance."

Almost at once, in answer to Ramon's prayers, Aida told us, his guardian angel manifested. And the heavenly warrior had brought some reinforcements of his own.

"There were three tall, muscular figures in shimmering white robes, each one brandishing a flaming sword,"

Ramon chuckled. "It didn't take long for those big guys from Heaven to scatter those angels of darkness back to their hellhole."

Ramon ran to take his sobbing wife in his arms and tell her that they were safe.

"At that very same moment," he said, "we awakened from our bizarre mutual dream—or whatever it was—clasping one another firmly."

His voice rising in excitement at the memory of the incredible experience, Ramon said that the truly eerie part of the dream drama was that he and Aida awakened in the middle of the bedroom, several feet away from the bed.

"I was holding Aida in my arms, just as I had been in the weird dream. Her hair was mussed and disheveled—and one of her pajama legs had been ripped off at the hip, just as it had been in the dream," Ramon said. "Aida gasped and touched a finger to my cheek. Blood was trickling down over my chin from a deep scratch in my cheek."

Aida nodded vigorously. "It is true. He had scratches and bruises all over his face, his chest, and his arms. And his pajamas were ripped in three places."

"And someone had turned on every single light in the bedroom and the bathroom," Ramon added.

"As if to keep away the angels of darkness with all the bright lights," Aida theorized.

To this day, Aida and Ramon still wonder if they had

somehow been drawn into a demonic dimension during the dream state—some shadow world, where grotesque night creatures dwell.

"I do know that my belief in guardian angels was intensified by the experience," Ramon said.

Aida nodded in reverent agreement, then added: "And I also know that after all these years, the torn and missing leg to my pajama bottoms has never turned up!"

The Netherlands

An angel saved him from drowning—then gave him a swimming lesson

Willy Zandvoort told us that he had received personalized instruction from a most remarkable swimming coach at his health club in Utrecht, Netherlands.

"In 1991, I was thirty-four years old, and I had still never learned how to swim in an effective style," Willy said. "When I was a little boy, an older cousin taught me how to stay afloat and kick and paddle in the small pond on our farm, but my style was not at all efficient. I would tire easily, and I looked like a harpooned whale threshing and splashing about. I was always embarrassed to have anyone see me in the water, and I avoided swimming parties as a teenager by protesting that I did not know how to swim."

When Willy moved to Utrecht, he joined a health club that had an indoor swimming pool, and he resolved to practice swimming until he had become more proficient in the water.

"But, once again, I was intimidated by the prowess of the other men in the club," he said. "There were expert swimmers who could move through the water as smoothly as eels and who could dive into the pool as confidently as seagulls snatching up fish. I didn't want to be in the way, so I spent most of the time sitting on the side of the pool, just dangling my feet in the water."

Although a sympathetic lifeguard gave him a few tips, Willy remained reluctant to paddle clumsily around the pool and block the paths of more accomplished swimmers.

And then Willy learned that there were few swimmers who used the pool after ten o'clock at night. "Neither was there any lifeguard on duty, but I discovered that I would quite likely have the pool nearly to myself for two hours until the club was locked up at midnight."

Willy enjoyed four or five nights of rigorous practice, and he believed that he was finally beginning to note some improvement in his style. But then came the night when the awful, paralyzing muscle cramp struck him.

"I was all alone in the pool! I had heard of such cramps

attacking swimmers, but I had not believed that they could really be so bad, so painful, so debilitating. It seemed as if I could not breathe or move a muscle, and I began to panic. I tried to relax, to stay somehow afloat."

Willy began choking on the water that he was swallowing. He thought that he would be found at midnight, floating facedown, drowned in the pool.

"Seemingly from out of nowhere, I felt strong arms holding me under my armpits. 'Relax,' said a voice in my ear. 'I've got you now. Stay calm. There's nothing to fear.'"

Soon the other swimmer had brought Willy to the shallow end and was kneading the cramped muscles.

"You saved my life," Willy told the man. "I cannot thank you enough. I was in a bad situation there."

Willy remembered his rescuer as a bit over six feet tall, with hair that was whitish-blond, "as if it had been bleached by the sun." The man had a warm smile and a friendly manner and a torso that was well developed, but not especially muscular.

"I will never forget his swimsuit," Willy said. "It was the most distinctive suit that I had ever seen. It was a bright, shiny silver color, as if it were made of polished aluminum or even stainless steel. And it seemed to fit his body like a second skin."

After Willy had rested, his new friend showed him a few moves that greatly improved his swimming stroke.

"He nodded his approval of my improved style, then he seemed almost to rise out of the water in a smooth, fluid movement and began to head toward the door of the pool," Willy said. "I called after him to wait, that I wanted at least to buy him a cup of coffee or tea, but he just waved over his shoulder and walked out the door."

Since the man didn't enter the locker and shower area but left directly by the outer door, Willy assumed that he must be one of the health club employees heading for the front office.

"After I got dressed, I expected to find him sitting in the outer area in a robe with a towel around his wet hair. But when I asked the lone employee still on duty who my friend was, he expressed complete ignorance of such a person—even when I described the distinctive shiny silver swimsuit that he wore."

Glancing at his watch and displaying obvious annoyance at Willy's insistent interrogation, the man impatiently stated that absolutely no one had come out of the pool door except for Willy since a few minutes before ten.

"You've been the only one splashing around in there for the last couple of hours," he told Willy. "It's been a really quiet night. Only a few guys in the weight room. Now can we go home?"

While it may have been a quiet night for the health

club attendant, Willy Zandvoort concluded, "I know that my guardian angel saved me from drowning—and taught me a few swimming tips at the same time. It was far from a quiet night for me!"

Norway

BROUGHT BACK FROM DEATH BY HER ANGEL— AND HER HUSBAND'S LOVE

In 1987, Krista Tjaden, who lives in a small town outside of Oslo, wrote to tell us about the awful night nearly fifteen years earlier when she died in her sleep. According to her understanding, it was only the intervention of her guardian angel and the love of her husband Jon that prevented her from passing to the other side.

Krista awakened one night in February, 1972, with a terrible pain that seemed to move from her abdominal region to her heart. "The pain was unbearable," she said, when she and Jon talked with us later. "I had a fleeting thought that I must be dying . . . and then I passed out."

At the same time, Jon lay dreaming that Krista had been shot by a thief as she walked on the street of a mountain village. "Police officers came running up, and they, in turn, shot the thug, but all that was too late to do Krista any good," he said. "In this awful dream, I saw them stretch Krista's body out on a park bench, and I ran to her and knelt by her side. With tears streaming down my cheeks, I kept shouting, 'Don't leave me! Oh, dear Krista, please don't leave me!' "

Krista said that in her reality she suddenly found herself walking through unfamiliar hilly and barren country.

"All around me was dark and dreary. I heard Jon shouting from somewhere in the darkness, 'Krista, please don't leave me.' His words kept repeating over and over again. I wanted to move, yet I could not. I wanted to answer him, but no sound came from my throat. I no longer had any control over my body."

It was at that frightening moment that Krista beheld a glowing figure of light manifesting before her. "I seemed to be able to make out these two beautiful blue eyes filled with pure love looking out at me from the bright light, but I could distinguish no other features. The brilliant light was in the shape of a human, but I can only describe the angel as being somehow composed of pure light."

Krista recalled that she seemed to hear a message from the angel that reverberated inside her very essence. "The angel said that it was not yet my time to cross to the other side. He said that Jon and I had things to learn together—and that I was to bear two children who would have a special mission to perform on Earth."

Dimly, Krista became aware of Jon sitting up in bed and turning her over on her back. "I felt just a trickle of life returning to my body. I found myself awake, my sleeping husband bending over me.

"Although Jon had turned me over and rubbed my neck, chest, and hands, he never once fully awakened despite his exertions. I lay there for quite some time, cautiously testing all my major body parts to see if everything was working again. At last I drifted into an uneasy sleep."

Jon, however, was still locked in his terrible nightmare about seeing his beloved Krista shot down by a hoodlum. "Krista was no longer lying still and cold on the park bench where the police officers had placed her," Jon said. "I saw her walking away from me into a strange and barren land. I tried to follow her, but I could not get past an invisible barrier. *I knew that she would leave me forever unless I could get her back.*"

Although Jon could not enter the dark, barren terrain, he could stand at the border and call to Krista to return. "I cried over and over again, 'My darling Krista, please don't leave me. Come back to me!'

"And suddenly this brilliant ball of light was leading her to me. 'Take her quickly,' a voice said from within the light. 'Take her by the hand and pull her back to Earth life.' "

The next thing Jon knew, he was bending over Krista in their bed, refusing to accept her death.

"I knew that I was in some kind of trancelike state when this beautiful angel appeared beside us and told me that I had been given a gift of healing from the heavenly host. The angel told me to turn Krista over on her back and to keep massaging her and to keep projecting thoughts of love to her."

When the alarm went off that morning, Krista awakened to find Jon holding her close to him.

"Jon told me about his dream and how the angel had told him to keep massaging me and sending me thoughts of love," she said. "We lay there for several minutes marveling over the strange manner in which dream states may be shared."

Finally Jon raised himself on an elbow and started to speak—then stopped, a ghastly pallor draining his features of their normal ruddiness. He reached over to the bedside table and handed Krista a mirror.

"One look shocked me," Krista said. "The skin under my eyes, around my mouth, and at the edges of my nostrils was blue. My flesh was cold and lifeless to the touch. My fingernails were blue, and so were my toenails and the palms of my hands. My whole body was rather unmanageable. Also, Jon noticed a place in my right eye where the white seemed to have congealed. Gradually, the bluish color left my fingernails and my palms, and I regained the use of my body after a few hours—but it took a week for all the blue on my face to go away. And I still have the spot in my eye after all this time.

"Once when a medical doctor saw the spot in my eye, he said that I must have come very close to death at some time for such a spot to have formed."

Krista and Jon went on to have two children, who at the time they contacted us were thirteen and eleven years old.

"Both Loren and Karla are very serious-minded childen who are already considering pursuing studies in social work or education," Jon said. "We know that they will soon be fulfilling the prophecy that Krista's angel made about their doing 'special work' here on Earth."

A prophecy, Krista added, that nearly cost their mother her life.

Persia

The Angel Played Cupid— and Defeated a Terrible Demon

Many have heard of the angel Raphael, but few are aware of the story of his appointment as matchmaker between Tobias, the son of Tobit, and the lovely maiden Sarah.

Raphael's Earth mission was made even more difficult by the fact that the nasty demon Asmodeus had become enamored of Sarah. This awful angel of darkness had already viciously dispensed with seven young men who had each very briefly become Sarah's husband—every one of them slaughtered by Asmodeus on the wedding night, before the marriage could be consummated. Although the demon himself had not yet attempted to defile the young woman's body or soul, he had made it clear to all powers and principalities that he considered Sarah his own.

Raphael assumed the name of Azarias and masqueraded as a kinsman to Tobit. The merchant welcomed him, then shared his great sorrow that as a result of his blindness he was unable to arrange a suitable union for his son with a woman of Israelite ancestry. "Azarias" told him that he would be pleased to serve as a guide and accompany Tobias to Media, where he might find a proper wife.

While on the long journey, Raphael took advantage of the travel time to teach Tobias rituals and prayers designed to ward off evil spirits, cure various diseases, and even remove the blight from Tobit's eyes. The angel on assignment appeared to all those humans he chanced to meet as an ordinary man possessed of extraordinary abilities and resourcefulness.

When they were nearing Ecbatana in Media, Raphael suggested that they stay at the home of Raguel, a kinsman, who had a daughter who would be eligible to become Tobias's wife. Not only was Sarah beautiful, the angel pointed out, but she was possessed of great common sense and a handsome dowry.

Tobias, however, had heard tales about Sarah, the "killer of husbands." He knew well that seven young men had dropped dead on their wedding night in the bridal chamber. He had been told that the demon Asmodeus loved Sarah and killed any man who approached her. He was the only son of his parents, and it would break their hearts if he were to meet such a grisly fate.

Raphael stood firm. He reminded Tobias that his father had commanded him to take a bride from his own ancestral tribe. The lovely Sarah fit the bill perfectly. And no reason to worry, the angel continued, the rituals and prayers that he had taught Tobias on the journey would protect him from the demon.

Continuing in his role as Tobias's kinsman, Raphael effectively guided the lad through the traditional marriage negotiations right up to the wedding night when Sarah and Tobias reverently entered the nuptial chamber. Although he had provided Tobias with a special incense to ward off Asmodeus, Raphael took no chances with any devilish interference. The powers of the angel of love and light were far superior to those of the creature of lust and darkness, and Raphael quickly overcame his demonic adversary, bound him securely, and carried him off to a desert in upper Egypt.

Raphael continued his masquerade as Azarias until he had brought the young couple safely home to the eagerly waiting Tobit. Then, after presiding over the healing of the merchant's eyes, the heavenly guide revealed his true identity.

"I am Raphael, one of the seven angels who stand before the Lord," he told them.

Tobias and Tobit immediately prostrated themselves before him, but Raphael assured them they need have no fear. Because the faithful Tobit had found favor with God, he, Raphael, had been assigned to heal him and to remove the demon who troubled Sarah.

"If I seemed to eat and drink with you," the angel explained, "it was only your imagination. Bless God, and tell all about his wonderful works. It is time now that I must return to the One who sent me."

After Raphael had spoken, he who had spent so many weeks living undetected among his human "kinsmen" disappeared before their astonished eyes.

The Philippines

HER GUARDIAN ANGEL
JOINED HER FOR LUNCH

Some years ago, a missionary friend named Mary told us that any doubts that she might have had about angels working directly in the lives of humans were immediately put to rest when she experienced her own angelic encounter.

It happened while she was in the Philippine Islands on mission work, during her very first visit to a private home. Perhaps the initial clue that her unseen guardian was at hand was provided when her hostess expressed surprise that the house's two giant guard dogs had not barked to announce the arrival of a stranger.

In the dining room, Mary was perplexed when her hostess proceeded to pull out two chairs—both, apparently, for Mary. Chuckling to herself, Mary reflected that she knew she had gained a few pounds, but certainly not enough to warrant two chairs.

Once Mary was seated, she smiled, observed the amenities, then noticed her gracious hostess setting another place at the table.

"It dawned on me that the other chair was quite likely for a family member or another guest who had not yet arrived," Mary said. "I was tempted to inquire who else was expected for lunch, but since I was not quite certain of Philippine customs, I thought it best not to."

Finally the hostess sat down and motioned for Mary to begin eating her lunch. Mary hesitated. The other chair remained empty. Wasn't it rude to begin eating when another guest was expected? However, when it was quite clear that the hostess was not at all reluctant to begin, Mary picked up her utensils and began.

After a few moments, their "getting to know you" conversation flowed easily. Mary found that she was enjoying herself and the wonderful company, yet she was very curious about why the hostess often looked at the empty chair throughout their lunch. At times, the hostess even appeared to be talking and gesturing to the chair as if it held an actual person.

"I'm afraid that I was just about convinced that my charming hostess might not be quite 'all there,' when I noticed that the full glass of milk that had been placed in front of the empty chair was almost empty," Mary said. "I know that my mouth must have dropped open, for there had been no one there to drink it."

Mary finally resolved to put thoughts of the empty chair and the disappearing milk out of her mind. The visit was otherwise going well.

A few more hours passed quickly, and Mary suddenly became concerned about overstaying her welcome.

As good-byes were being said at the door, Mary was again perplexed by her hostess when she put one arm around Mary's shoulders and the other around thin air.

"How nice it was, Mary, that your friend came with you," the courteous woman smiled.

Mary was stunned, and felt her knees buckle.

"Then it all became very clear to me," she told us. "Before I had started out for the woman's house, I had prayed extra hard for protection because I had heard that she lived in a rough neighborhood. I glanced back at the chair at the table and the nearly empty glass of milk at the place setting, and I thanked God for this extraordinary evidence that my prayer had been answered. I had been truly blessed to have had an angel companion who joined me for lunch."

An Angel Took Him Through Solid Walls in Locked Rooms

On a bright spring day in 1951, Rodolfo Fermin squirmed in his seat in the sixth grade room of a public school in Manila. As if the schoolwork were not difficult enough, his teacher had given him a special assignment—keeping an eye on a fellow student named Cornelio.

Normally, the task would have been easy enough, but Cornelio had gained the reputation of being the school's worst truant. Rodolfo looked nervously at Cornelio across the aisle. He seemed to be absorbed in a book.

Rodolfo leaned over to pick up a pencil that had fallen to the floor. He straightened up, then looked across the aisle again. *Cornelio's desk was empty. He had vanished once again from the midst of a classroom with all of its doors and windows securely locked.*

Cornelio Closa had become a vexing problem for the school and for his parents. Time after time his exasperated teachers would report him truant, and Cornelio's outraged father would attempt to discipline the boy. But as often as this happened, Cornelio would somehow manage to disappear from closed and locked rooms.

FIFTEEN YEARS OR so later, in the late 1960s, Vicente Maliwang of United Press International interviewed Cornelio in Manila, where he now worked as an electrician and lived with his wife and children. According to Cornelio, when he was a sixth grader he encountered a most remarkable entity that opened up a whole new dimension of reality for him.

The being appeared to Cornelio as a beautiful girl, about his age, who was dressed completely in white. Her long blond hair hung to her waist. She walked barefoot— yet she seemed not to walk at all. Rather, she appeared to float several inches off the ground.

She had held out her hand to Cornelio, and after he clasped it in his own he felt that he had somehow changed. He felt so very much lighter, and it seemed as though he, too, could float several inches off the ground.

He described his first journey with the beautiful, blond angelic being as "dreamlike." The strange places that they visited did not remain in his memory for very long.

During their next journey together, Cornelio paid closer attention to his surroundings. The places they went seemed real enough—even though no one seemed to pay any attention to them. Cornelio later deduced that he and his ethereal companion were invisible to others.

At first Cornelio confided in no one, but his prolonged absences from school soon raised anger and embarrassment in his parents.

Even though his teachers took extra precautions to guarantee Cornelio's attendance in the classroom, no locked door or close surveillance could deter him from leaving with his beautiful angelic companion. Just as soon as she manifested beside him in the classroom, Cornelio and she would first become invisible, then leave through closed doors.

After his repeated absences from school became a matter of general disturbance, Cornelio was finally restricted to his parents' home.

The Closa family locked the doors to Cornelio's room and kept a careful watch on all the exits, but such precautions did nothing to stop the lovely ethereal being from visiting him; nor did they deter the strange couple from leaving the house to travel wherever they wished.

Cornelio's father swore in an affidavit that, on several occasions, he locked his son in his room, only to return later to find the room empty. He had no explanation for how Cornelio could possibly have left the totally secure house.

Eventually Cornelio grew tired of being locked up, tested, and studied, and he told his father about the beautiful blond girl and the strange walks that he took with her.

Although the boy's description of the lovely girl sounded as though he were describing an angel of light, Rev. Lester Sumrall, who preached at the Knox Memorial Church in Manila, wondered how any true, conscientious angel could have taken Cornelio away from his studies, encouraged him to be truant, and caused his parents and teachers extreme concern and confusion.

Whether Cornelio's multidimensional companion was an angel of light or an angel of darkness and discord masquerading as a lovely young girl to ensnare the boy, she was never seen by Cornelio again after Reverend Sumrall uttered a brief prayer of exorcism: "In the name of Jesus, go away!"

Puerto Rico

HER GUARDIAN ANGEL
SAVED HER FROM DATE RAPE

Some years ago, Isadora Bayena, a young woman from Arecibo, Puerto Rico, presented us with an account of a dramatic angelic manifestation which she experienced when she was two months shy of seventeen and uninitiated in the ways of a man with a woman.

"I begged my parents to allow me to travel to San Juan to celebrate New Year's Eve with my older brother Alejandro," Isadora said. "He had invited me to come stay in his apartment in the city when he was home for Christmas, and I felt very grown-up to be thought worthy by my twenty-two-year-old brother of visiting his place in San Juan."

But when Isadora arrived at Alejandro's apartment, he apologized and explained that two of his college friends had arrived unexpectedly and there was no longer any room for her to stay with him.

"My heart sank. I felt so dejected and miserable," Isadora said. "I was certain that Alejandro would now order me to go back home."

Instead, her brother said that he had arranged for her to sleep in the apartment of one of his friends during her holiday stay in San Juan. Isadora had heard Alejandro speak of Luis Murillo, and she knew that he was an "older man" of twenty-four.

"Now I was faced with a dilemma," Isadora said. "I had given my parents my sacred word that I would be a 'good girl' during my visit to the big city. I knew that Luis was a handsome man who was probably very experienced with members of the opposite sex. Would it be possible to remain a 'good girl' while I stayed alone with him in his apartment? I knew that I should get back on the next bus home to Arecibo, but I really wanted to celebrate New Year's Eve in the big city."

Alejandro assured his sister that Luis Murillo was a perfect gentleman and that he had two bedrooms in his apartment. "He will treat you as if you were his own sister," Alejandro promised. "Or he knows that I will break his neck. We will just agree that we will not tell Mother and Father that you are staying with Luis instead of with me."

Isadora moved into the spare bedroom in Luis Murillo's apartment and found that the man was, indeed, a perfect gentleman. She also found that there was a great deal of warmth and affection developing between them.

For the first two nights, Isadora retired discreetly to her own bedroom after she and Luis had spent the early part of the evening at Alejandro's apartment.

On New Year's Eve, they all went out dancing and drinking, and Isadora was even allowed to have some wine under her brother's watchful eye.

"Shortly after midnight, after we had watched the fireworks over the ocean, I knew that I must get home to bed," Isadora said. "I was not yet a party animal. That I had truly discovered for certain."

She was unaware that Luis had also returned to the apartment until she felt him lie down beside her on the bed.

"He told me that for two nights he had kept his word to Alejandro that I should remain a 'good girl,' but that on this particular night, New Year's Eve, his masculine drive refused to be quieted."

Isadora was stunned when Luis suddenly rolled her over on her back and pinned her hands to the mattress with his own sweating palms.

"What . . . what are you doing, Luis?" she gasped as she

was rudely shaken into startled wakefulness. She struggled beneath him, fighting to free herself from his weight and his strength. "Luis . . . you promised me. You promised Alejandro!"

Luis's breath was coming in short gasps as his passion rose. "I can't take it any longer. I want you now!"

Isadora began to weep. "Not this way, Luis. I want to be able to choose the time . . . the place . . . and the man."

"What's wrong with me?" he demanded.

"There was nothing wrong with you—until now!" Isadora screamed at him. "Luis, this is rape!"

Suddenly the room was filled with a softly glowing light. Isadora and Luis were astonished to see the Virgin Mary appear at the side of the bed.

Isadora recalled the apparition vividly. "Blue cloth partially shielded her face, and she never removed her eyes from mine. Luis rolled over on his back, all sexual desire instantly drained from his body. He, too, had been raised Catholic, and though he had abandoned some of its more ritualistic aspects of worship, the figure of the Holy Mother moved him deeply.

"Luis began to weep, deeply, in great wracking sobs, begging my forgiveness, the forgiveness of the Virgin Mary, the forgiveness of God. The image of Mary remained at the bedside for three or four minutes before it slowly faded away."

The next morning over breakfast, Isadora and Luis

discussed the powerful vision and its many ramifications for their lives.

"After talking about it for several hours, we more or less both decided that it had not been the *actual* Virgin Mary, the Mother of Jesus, who had manifested in the bedroom to smile down on me, but the personification of the ideal of virginity," Isadora said. "Luis believed that my guardian angel had chosen the particular symbol of the Virgin Mary with which to manifest, because the heavenly being had known that such an image would have great impact on him.

"Luis also said that he would truly respect my sovereignty as a young woman and that I would certainly remain a 'good girl' for the remainder of my visit in San Juan. Neither Alejandro nor my guardian angel would have to worry about him losing his perfect manners again."

Saudi Arabia

ANGEL GABRIEL GAVE HIM
THE WORDS TO ESTABLISH ISLAM

According to those who adhere to the Islamic faith, Islam begins not with Muhammad in seventh-century Arabia, but with God. The word itself—*Islam*—means the peace that comes from surrendering one's life to God. Muslims' word *Allah* is exactly the same as our word *God*—not *a god*, but the One God.

The Muslims also place much faith in the prophets, whose ancestry as recorded in the Old Testament stems basically from the eldest son of Noah. This son, Shem, had descendants from whom Abraham came. Abraham married Sarah, and then Hagar, because Sarah had borne him no son. Hagar did bear him a son, Ishmael. Shortly after that, an angel told Abraham and Sarah they would have a son, though they were in their nineties. Even though they found this announcement incredible, Sarah did bear a son, whom they were to call Isaac. Sarah then demanded that Hagar and her son Ishmael be banished from the tribe.

According to the Qur'an, Ishmael went to the place where Mecca was to rise. His descendants flourished in Arabia. From them came Muhammad and the Islamic faith, whose followers are known as Muslims. The descendants of Isaac, however, remained in Palestine and gave rise to the Hebrews—later called the Jews.

MUHAMMAD WAS BORN into the leading tribe of Mecca, the Quaraysh, in approximately 570 A.D., at a time of harsh and chaotic world conditions. He was adopted by his uncle, as both of his parents died when he was young. It is said that the angels of God opened Muhammad's heart and filled it with light. He was of a gentle and kind disposition and was extremely sensitive and compassionate. He was touched by human suffering and was always ready to help others, especially those who were poor, sickly, or weak.

Muhammad didn't fit into life around him. His peers were lawless and immoral. He turned inward.

When Muhammad reached maturity, he became a merchant. When he was in his mid-twenties his work aligned him with a widow, Khadijah. She was very impressed with Muhammad's prudence, integrity, and kindness, which stood out against the barbaric manners of his peers. Eventually, their working relationship grew from friendship to love, and although she was fifteen years older than he, they married—and were very happy in every respect. "God comforted him through her, for she made his burden light."

Prophets often have a "burden for humankind." Muhammad began a fifteen-year period of preparation for his ministry. He would go to a mountain on the edge of Mecca and seek solitude in a cave. As it is said, his "great fiery heart" was reaching out for God, trying to understand the mysteries of good and evil and the painful condition of those who were suffering and heavy of heart.

Muhammad would hold vigils that frequently lasted all night long. He continued his vigils unceasingly until he got an answer. Muhammad became convinced that there was only one God, not many, and that this was a great God. He became electrified with the knowledge that there is no God but God.

One night as Muhammad lay on the floor of the cave,

an angel appeared to him in the form of a man. The angel said one word: "Proclaim!" Muhammad responded honestly, telling the angel that he was not a proclaimer. The angel persisted, saying: "Proclaim in the name of your Lord who created Man from blood coagulated! Proclaim: Your Lord is wondrous kind, Who teaches by the pen, Things men knew not, being blind."

In a trancelike state, Muhammad was terrified. He hurried home to Khadijah and told her of his experience. He felt the angel's words had branded his soul, and he told her that he had either become a prophet—or a madman! He must have been filled with a great light because his wife became his first convert. From that time on, Muhammad's life was no longer his own. The angel returned to him often and always commanded him to proclaim. He was to preach the words given him by the angel.

The words were given to Muhammad in segments over twenty-three years through voices that sounded to him at first like reverberating bells. Gradually they condensed into a single voice that identified itself as the Angel Gabriel. Muhammed often went into a state of ecstacy—a complete trance wherein he would be visibly altered. His appearance would change dramatically to any who might see him in this state, in which he received the teachings from Gabriel. Muhammed would say that the words physically assaulted him as if they were heavy and solid.

The words that Muhammad exclaimed in these trance-like states were memorized by his followers, who wrote them down on anything they could find—bones, leaves, bark, and scraps of parchment—in order to preserve their accuracy.

THE QUR'AN AS the Word of God given by the Angel Gabriel is central to the lives of Muslims. Large portions of it are memorized by young children. It is the governing factor in making decisions and in interpreting any event. The Qur'an is also a collection of maxims that are meditated on in private, or recited aloud in prayer.

It is interesting that when Muhammad began his ministry and was teaching the words and laws given him by the angel, he was met with bitterness and persecution. He taught of one God in a pagan, materialistic world. He continued always to teach and adjure listeners to abandon their evil ways and prepare for the day of reckoning. Eventually, he won over nearly all of Arabia, though at times he had to flee cities because of the resentment and hostility shown him. He evolved into a loved, honored, revered, and obeyed statesman, unifying Arabia from a fragmented, uncivilized, uncouth country to a land touched with the spirit of cooperation. People flocked from all over to see him and learn from him. The Angel

Gabriel gave Muhammad the words that have led to the Islamic religion, which today counts one fifth of the world's population among its followers.

When a Man dies, they who survive him ask what property he has left behind: The angel who bends over the dying man asks what good deeds he has sent before him.

—*THE QUR'AN*

Sicily

HER ANGELS BROUGHT HER TO THE WEEPING MADONNA TO BE CURED

A friend of ours, who in 1965 emigrated from Sicily to the United States as a young woman of twenty, told us how, as a teenager, she was brought by her angels to the statue of the weeping Madonna in Siracusa to be cured of asthma.

"Since I was a small child, I had suffered through days when I could hardly breathe," Lina Grisetti said. "When I was thirteen, I had a vision of two angels in glowing white gowns who told me that I must visit the statue of the weeping Madonna. They promised me that I would be cured of my asthmatic condition after I had made such a pilgrimage.

"My uncles and aunts were skeptical of my vision, but after I traveled with my parents from our home in Ragusa and knelt before the statue of the weeping Madonna, my asthma started at once to get better and better. I haven't had an attack now in over thirty years."

WE WERE CURIOUS to learn more about the weeping Madonna, and Lina seemed eager to answer our questions.

The statue itself was just a foot-high Madonna cast in hollow plaster and painted with bright blotches of cheap paint. In her crudely shaped fingers, the Madonna held a bleeding heart painted in red and edged in gold. She was precisely like thousands of Madonnas sold throughout the country for a few lire.

This particular statue became a wedding present for Antionetta and Angelo Iannuso, who were married in Siracusa in the spring of 1953.

"Antionetta was a very religious Catholic girl who carefully followed the instructions of the church," Lina said. "Angelo, however, was a farm laborer who was an admitted Communist sympathizer."

After a few months of marriage, Antionetta became pregnant and almost at once began to experience terrible headaches.

"Her vision dimmed, and she found it difficult to perform even the simplest of household tasks," Lina said. "She prayed devoutly to the Madonna to end her pain."

On the morning of August 29, 1953, Antionetta was afflicted with a painful seizure. Her abdomen twisted with pain, and her eyes clouded.

"It was then that a beautiful light seemed to appear around her, and she could hear the heavenly sound of a choir of angels singing," Lina continued. "A voice told her to behold the statue of the Madonna—and Antionetta saw tears streaming down her face."

Antionetta dashed from the room, forgetting her pain, shouting that the little Madonna was weeping.

Her mother and sister-in-law came to investigate and discovered tears so plentiful that they were flowing down the Madonna's face and over into the hand that held the heart.

Even the skeptical Angelo witnessed the torrent of tears.

A neighbor of the Iannuso family, not wishing to be taken in by a phenomenon stemming from natural causes or unconscious fraud, removed the statue from the wall in an effort to discover some rational explanation for the apparent miracle.

"The man later told a newspaper reporter that he was unable to find any moisture on the wall," Lina told us. "Later, he unscrewed the statue from its base and found that it was thoroughly dry on the inside. A few seconds after he had dismantled the Madonna, two pearllike tears glistened in her eyes."

LINA SAID THAT when the news spread throughout Italy, thousands of people hurried to see the weeping statue.

Further credence was given to the statue when the Siracusa police removed the Madonna to their headquarters for safety. As the squad car moved through the streets, the patrolman who carefully held the statue on his lap discovered that his jacket was drenched with tears.

A skeptical detective caught several of the Madonna's tears in a vial and brought them to the police laboratory for analysis, and the lab director later decreed them to be human tears.

According to Lina, the unusual healing power of the weeping Madonna had manifested itself immediately. From the moment when Antionetta had first glimpsed the tears, her painful seizures were gone. Her vision cleared and her thudding headaches became a thing of the past.

Other cures quickly followed. The crippled and the sick gathered before the weeping statue to be brushed by a cloth moistened with the Madonna's tears.

The Madonna's tears ceased to flow on the fourth day.

———

ONE MONTH LATER the little statue was carried through the streets of Siracusa at the head of a procession of thirty thousand people. The Madonna was taken to a former railroad shed and devoutly encased in a glass structure capped with a bronze cross.

"And, of course, the healings continued," Lina said. "I was but one of the thousands who have been blessed in some way by the angels and the Madonna."

At the time she visited the statue in 1958, Lina told us, masses were being said throughout the day by a local priest, assisted by Antionetta's husband Angelo, who had forsaken Communist doctrine for Catholicism. (Hopeful that their community might become the Italian Lourdes, the citizens of Siracusa purchased a twelve-acre site and in 1970 began construction of a teardrop-shaped shrine for the statue; the shrine has room for twenty thousand pilgrims within its four-hundred-foot-high walls.)

"By 1958, more than one hundred bishops and archbishops and several cardinals had visited the shrine," Lina said. "The glass-walled case was surrounded by dozens of crutches and braces that had been left there by the cured. When I saw those symbols of suffering that had been discarded by others who had come to the weeping Madonna before me, I knew that my angels had brought me to the right place to receive my own healing."

Spain

THOUSANDS WITNESS GIRL'S CONVERSATION WITH AN ANGEL

In August 1965, a crowd of nearly a thousand people gathered in a peaceful grove outside the isolated village of San Sebastian de Garabandal, Spain. Some had come to pray, some to be healed, others to satisfy their curiosity, still others to mock—but all were there to hear a prophetic message from Conchita Gonzalez, a pretty, sixteen-year-old farm girl who had allegedly been conducting conversations with St. Michael the Archangel.

"She comes from the house," whispered an old woman.

A journalist checked his watch. Nearly midnight.

Conchita walked slowly to the grove, seemingly unaware of the crowd that had gathered to hear and observe her.

Within a few moments, she threw back her head and appeared to be speaking to someone who could not be seen by the assembled throng.

During her ten-minute "conversation," a medical doctor emerged from the crowd and checked her pulse. "It is normal," he told a representative from a wire service. Conchita did not appear to have noticed the physician's actions.

Minutes later, the teenager shook her head sharply, then smiled benevolently at the crowd.

"To whom did you speak?" asked individual voices from within the mass of humanity gathered to observe her—each person desiring the information for his or her own particular reason.

"I have spoken with the Archangel St. Michael," Concita told the eagerly waiting assemblage. "He gave me an important message of wondrous things to come."

With those words of impending import, Concita walked slowly home, once again aloof to the shouted demands and questions of the excited multitude.

THE HEAVENLY DISCOURSES in Garabandal began in 1961, when Conchita and three of her friends first saw the angel. After he had identified himself as Michael the Archangel, he told the girls that the Virgin Mary would soon appear with him.

On the evening of Sunday, July 2, 1961, Conchita and her companions beheld Michael in the company of another majestic angel that could have been his heavenly twin. Between them stood a beautiful young woman with long dark-brown hair. She wore a long, brilliant white dress under a flowing blue mantle. Around her head was a crown that appeared to be fashioned of small, sparkling gold stars. The young Spanish girls had no doubt that this lovely lady was the Virgin Mary.

During the next nineteen months, the Virgin and Michael appeared to Conchita and the three other farm girls some two thousand times, often in several visitations a day, though not always to all four of them at once.

Witnesses observed the girls being levitated in their ecstasy, as if to rise to kiss the holy figures. Sometimes the girls were seen to be lowered slowly backwards to the ground, their backs ramrod straight. Once a large crowd even saw them walking in the air.

IN NOVEMBER 1965, the Virgin appeared to Conchita for the last time. She admonished the teenager to continue to do good works for all people—and then she was gone.

Conchita stood in the grove outside the village for a

few moments longer, reflecting on all that had happened to her in the past four years. She told observers that while she knew that she would no longer see the angel and the Virgin, she would feel their presence all the rest of her life.

Turkey

"You are your brother's keeper"

Mustafa Ozal, who now resides in Boston, told us of the angelic encounter that he experienced as a young man in Ankara, Turkey.

"My father had been killed in an automobile accident in 1947," he said. "When Mother became ill in 1951, my older sister was already married, but my younger brother Suleiman and I lived at home. Mother's condition steadily worsened, and she knew that she would soon be joining our father in paradise.

"One night, just a few days before she died, Mother

called me to her bedside and asked me to take a vow that I would look after Suleiman. I had just turned twenty. I had a good job and was taking some university courses. Suleiman was seventeen, quite lazy, and inclined to run with a wild crowd of young men."

Mustafa said that because of his great love for his mother he made a promise to keep an eye on Suleiman. "But I knew that I would have my hands full looking after the rascal, and I somewhat resented having such responsibility placed on my head."

Two months after their mother had passed away, Suleiman had established a regular routine of late hours carousing with his companions. He soon lost his part-time job, and he began to neglect his studies at the trade school. Mustafa urged his brother to change his reckless ways and take life more seriously, but he made no real effort to curb Suleiman's destructive lifestyle.

"I had more or less turned my back on Suleiman and concentrated more on ignoring him than on attempting to alter his worthless ways," Mustafa admitted. "My dream was to go to America and become a citizen of the United States. I did not wish Suleiman's bad habits to block my plans for advancement."

One night at about midnight, Mustafa was awakened by the sound of someone calling his name. "I rolled over in bed, and I was astonished to behold a magnificent angelic being in a long, flowing white robe standing beside me. The angel seemed to be glowing so bright that I had to shield my eyes."

And then, in a very clear and authoritative voice, the being told Mustafa that Suleiman was in great danger.

"You made a promise to your mother," the angel reminded him. "You vowed that you would take care of your brother. Know this, Mustafa, you are your brother's keeper! You must go at once to the place where you know he gambles and bring him home. He is in very great danger."

Having delivered the warning, the majestic being disappeared and left Mustafa trembling in awe and fear. "I knew that I could not disregard such an admonition, so I got dressed and prepared to set out at once for the den of ill repute where I knew Suleiman and his boisterous crowd hung out.

"At first Suleiman was angry and defiant when I walked into the place," he recalled. "His rowdy bunch of friends hooted at me and shouted insults, but I managed to draw Suleiman apart from them so that we could talk privately. Strangely enough, he became very quiet and attentive when I told him about the remarkable angelic visitation that I had experienced. And when I stressed that the angel had said that he was in great danger, Suleiman agreed to leave with me."

The next day at work, Mustafa learned that a quarrel

had escalated to a knife fight among the gamblers at the den frequented by Suleiman.

"Two of Suleiman's friends had been badly injured, and another had been killed," Mustafa said. "If the angelic being had not reminded me of my responsibility to my brother and my promise to my mother, he might have been a casualty or a fatality of the fight. Suleiman experienced a dramatic change in his lifestyle that day, and in five years we were both able to come to America to establish new lives."

Uganda

Delivered from an African Death Curse

Beatrice Gompu from Uganda was a student in a creative writing class that Brad taught in a small midwestern college. Her father was a very wealthy man back in her home village, and because she was the favorite child of her father's favorite wife, she had been allowed to travel to the United States to further her education. Beatrice and Brad became good friends, and she often visited his home and his family for long, metaphysical discussions over cups of tea.

Although she had attended a Christian school and taken the Christian name of Beatrice, she was well versed in the traditional spiritual practices of her people. "Magic," she once explained, "is completely integrated into all aspects of our life in my region of Uganda. Magic is always with us—alive, invigorating, but often very deadly."

Beatrice said that her people's belief in good and evil spirits correlated very closely to concepts of many other religions. When the missionaries delineated the concept of angels, she identified them as the benevolent spirits of nature. As she learned more about the world's religions, she began more and more to blend the concepts of guardian angels, benevolent nature beings, and the Hindu portraits of the *devas*, or "radiant beings."

During one of their conversations, Beatrice told Brad the story of how one of these radiant beings had rescued her father from a deadly curse that had been set upon him.

MARTIN GOMPU HAD been suffering from a lengthy illness that no practitioner of Western medicine in the region was able to cure. Eventually, the family acknowledged that a business competitor had set a curse upon him.

"Father was a wealthy man with eight daughters. Soon prospective sons-in-law would increase his wealth by bringing their own fortunes to the family," Beatrice said. "Only the jackal Saja was jealous enough and evil enough to try to kill Father. However, Saja knew that he was too weak to fight Father physically, so he secured the services of the most powerful witch doctor in the area and paid him to cast a terrible curse upon him."

For six awful years, Gompu's powerful physique managed to withstand the debilitating effects of the curse, until at last he was able to find a witch doctor endowed with the power to lift the sickness from him.

Ironically, Beatrice observed, Saja's nephew and only male heir, Amisi, was her brother John's best friend. "I always felt that the little snake was only trying to ingratiate himself with my family, because he knew that one day he and John would be the two central figures in the village. I am certain that his greedy mind envisioned a coalition between the two most powerful families."

Meanwhile, the sinister Saja was unrelenting in his hatred of Beatrice's father. After an extensive search of the outlying villages, he managed to find an even more powerful witch doctor to set yet another curse upon Martin Gompu.

On a night of thunder and lightning and wind, a night made for the working of black magic and evil, the terrible ordeal reached its climax.

Beatrice's father had been gone for several days on a business trip, and on the evening of the violent storm, the family heard chanting outside their home. When they looked out the windows, they were astonished to see Saja and his fierce-looking witch doctor standing in the pouring rain. A small crowd of men had gathered to observe the eerie drama.

Saja's cackle sounded above the noise of the storm as he shouted that this time he would kill Martin Gompu.

Mocking voices from the crowd challenged Saja that if he failed this time, he was a worm, not a man.

"With shocked, incredulous eyes, my family watched helplessly as Saja and his witch doctor performed the dark rites necessary to bring about the destruction of the head of our household," Beatrice said, shuddering at the memory. "A young goat was brought into the magic circle, and I must confess that I screamed when the witch doctor slit its throat. Everyone knew that as soon as the goat was slain in sacrifice, something horrible would happen to my father."

And all during the dark ceremony, Beatrice remembered, the snake Amisi stood with a pitiful expression, seeming to plead with the Gompu family that he was helpless to come to their aid.

Beatrice began to pray, asking all the angels of light that the missionaries said were protecting them to stand guard over her father. "I somehow felt within my very soul that I had always known the presence of guardian spirits in my life, and I begged them to manifest to protect my father on his homeward journey."

Saja's witch doctor tossed the carcass of the sacrificial goat on the fire and made his final pronouncement of that night of storm and dark magic. "No one is to touch the goat's flesh," he roared at the assembled crowd of onlookers and the members of Saja's family. "If any of you do so, the deadly curse will be upon you!"

Beatrice and her family expected her father's return by ten o'clock. The awful curse was levied at nine.

Soon it was eleven. Then midnight.

"We maintained our silent, prayerful vigil, but we had begun to fear the worst," Beatrice said.

It was two forty-five when they heard at last the sputtering of the family automobile. Beatrice's father had to be alive, for he was the only one of the men who had gone on the business trip who knew how to drive a car!

Martin Gompu and his companions were soaked, splattered with mud, and completely exhausted—but they were alive.

"As we gathered to hug and kiss him, Father explained that a strange thing had occurred as they approached the main bridge over the river. A man with a bright lantern had jumped in front of the car with his arms outstretched, as if warning them. To avoid striking the man, Father had swerved into the ditch.

"When the men got out of the car, the man with the lantern had disappeared, but they discovered that the bridge had collapsed into the river. If they had continued on, they would undoubtedly have plunged into the rushing water and drowned. I knew in my heart that the man with the lantern had been an angel manifesting in answer to my prayer."

With the bridge out, her father explained, they had to take the long route home. That was why they were so late.

Beatrice asked her father if he knew what time the man with the lantern appeared to warn them.

He smiled and replied that he had happened to glance at his wristwatch just before the stranger appeared on the road. It was exactly nine o'clock.

"Father was shocked when I told him that was the very moment that Saja's new witch doctor had slit the goat's throat and sent a death curse flying toward him," Beatrice said.

Beatrice knew that her prayer to the benevolent beings of light had been answered. A bright, glowing entity had manifested on the road and prevented her father and his companions from drowning in the river.

But the heavenly guardians had accomplished a twist on the deeds of the evildoers that she could never have envisioned.

The next morning, Amisi was found dead. In his mouth was a piece of goat meat. He could not resist having one little bite of the sacrificial animal that the witch doctor had thrown on the fire. And so his greed had transferred the deadly effects of the curse from Beatrice's father to Amisi and his own family.

The United States

GRAY ROBE, GUARDIAN ANGEL OF RED VALLEY

Consistent among the tribes of Native Americans is the belief that each person has an individual guardian spirit or guide. For two centuries, the Navajo in the old Red Valley region of Arizona near Tonalca have testified that they have been assisted in times of peril by the manifestation of the guardian entity that they have come to know as Gray Robe.

Oral traditions tell of the young Navajo named Black Hat who was traveling alone by starlight along the Red Valley Trail when his pony reared sharply in alarm at the form of a figure in gray standing just off the path. Black Hat saw that the man in the gray robe was motioning to him to follow him through the heavy sagebrush. Deciding to heed the stranger's beckoning hand, he nudged his pony off the trail.

Before the figure vanished, he had indicated one particular rocky ridge. There, at its base, Black Hat discovered a Navajo lying unconscious. The man's leg was broken.

Gathering dry sagebrush, Black Hat started a signal fire, which attracted a number of Navajo who lived in the area.

When the injured man regained consciousness, he said that he had been thrown from his horse. Everyone agreed that he would have died had Gray Robe not led Black Hat to find him.

Some local legends identify the mysterious benefactor in the gray robe as the spirit of a certain Father Esdalante who, together with other priests, survived a bitter winter in the 1770s thanks to a small band of Navajo who shared their meager rations with them. As the folds of his long gray robe flapped along his lean frame in the cold, swirling wind, Father Esdalante blessed the place and its people and called on God's eternal protection for the Navajo in the Red Valley.

Others say that rather than being the spirit of Father Esdalante, Gray Robe is actually an angel who answered the priest's fervent prayer to Heaven to provide a guardian for the compassionate people of the Red Valley.

————

IN ANOTHER INSTANCE, Gray Robe is said to have saved the life of a crippled Navajo woman who was alone and starving in an isolated hogan. According to the story, the benevolent being appeared at her door and motioned for her to follow him. Miraculously, she rose on her crippled legs and walked with him for nearly a mile along an abandoned horse trail. Gray Robe vanished just as a Navajo couple appeared to rescue the old woman. They could give no explanation as to why they yielded to impulse and decided to go home by way of the old trail instead of their usual route.

NOT LONG AGO, Gray Robe rescued two lost sisters who had wandered too far from their summer sheep camp near Red Lake. The sudden onset of a blinding sandstorm made a search for the lost girls nearly impossible.

By nightfall, all but one man, a white trader named Joe Lee, had given up the hunt. He was just approaching a spring when he saw the form of a tall man in a gray robe holding out both arms to him.

Lee blinked in astonishment, then spotted the two little girls walking just a short distance behind the man in gray. When the man seemed certain that Lee had seen the sisters, he disappeared.

Later, the girls said that Gray Robe had led them to a cave where they might have safe refuge against the storm. He had blessed them and prayed over them in the manner of Christian missionaries.

The trader had often heard the tales about Gray Robe, but he had simply attributed them to folklore. He was satisfied with an elderly Navajo's statement that although no one knew exactly *who* or *what* Gray Robe was, everyone knew for certain that he was their protector, their guardian spirit.

California
HIS UNSEEN GUARDIAN PROTECTED HIM IN TRAVELING FROM TOKYO TO LOS ANGELES

Twice in his life, A. R. Thompson has been saved by the voice of an angelic guide, and he is convinced that there are benevolent beings that guide our lives—if we will but listen.

Thompson first became aware of his guardian angel's presence in 1947 when he was being discharged from the army and processed home from the occupation forces in

Japan. He was offered his choice of traveling by ship or airplane, and since he had been separated from his family in the States for so long, he unhesitatingly chose to travel by plane.

Six hours before he was scheduled to depart from the Tokyo airport, he lay on his bunk and thought lovingly of the family that he had not seen for two years.

"It would be wiser to go home by ship," a voice from out of nowhere suddenly told him.

Thompson jumped out of his bunk and looked around him. The barracks was empty—yet the voice sounded as though it had been speaking directly into his ear.

Assured that he was alone, he lay back down on his bunk.

The voice spoke again, sounding so clear and natural that Thompson would have sworn there was someone standing next to him. *"You should go home by ship."*

Thompson had heard of people who claimed to hear voices from other spheres, but he had always dismissed such stories as delusions or exaggerations. He sat for a few moments on the edge of his bunk, attempting to steady his nerves. And then the eerie thought struck him: What if this was a genuine mystical experience and he was truly receiving heavenly advice from an angel? Should he heed the unseen speaker?

He lay back on his bunk, trying his best to convince himself that he was just overtired.

"Please believe me! It will be better for you if you go home by ship."

That did it! Thompson figured that three times was enough for the hardiest of skeptics.

He went straight to his commanding officer and informed him that he had changed his mind. He wished to return by ship.

"All right," the officer scowled. "I'll try."

As it turned out, there was a great deal of resistance to Thompson's sudden and unexpected request, and several times he felt like forgetting the bother. Each time, though, something checked him, and he stood firm in his resolve.

Finally the change in travel plans was confirmed, and Thompson's commanding officer booked him aboard a homeward-bound ship scheduled to leave Tokyo the next week.

Three hours later the plane on which Thompson had been scheduled to leave for the States crashed during takeoff, killing all on board.

Thompson was terribly shaken by the grim news and gave thanks for the strange warning process that had managed to keep him off the plane.

A COUPLE OF years later, while visiting his mother in Los Angeles, Thompson was invited to a friend's home for dinner. Little did he know when he accepted the invitation to meet the man's family and wax nostalgic about college days that he would be inviting his guardian angel to manifest once again.

To get to his friend's home in the San Fernando Valley, Thompson had to go by way of Cahuenga Pass, a busy speedway that was nearly always clogged with traffic on weekends. Anticipating difficulties and delays, he allowed himself a full hour for travel.

True to his concern, he soon found cars lined up bumper to bumper, and he became excruciatingly aware of the minutes ticking away. When he could finally pull away from the slow-moving mass of automobiles, he pushed hard on the accelerator.

He had gone no more than a mile when he distinctly heard a voice speaking in his ear: *"You had better stop the car."*

Thompson gave a start. The instant that he heard the voice his mind was filled with memories of the tragic plane crash at the Tokyo airport. Even so, he resisted the command to stop the car in the middle of one of the busiest freeways in Los Angeles.

"You had better stop the car immediately!"

Thompson thought once more of the horrible plane crash, and he began to slow down.

A stream of angrily honking cars roared past him as he drew off to the side of the road and stopped his automobile.

"All right," he wondered aloud. "What am I to do now?"

"Get a tow truck. Do not drive this car any farther."

Thompson decided that he might as well obey his invisible advisor. He turned off the car—the car that seemed to be running just fine—and walked to a pay phone. He found the number of a garage in the area and requested a tow truck.

Later, when the mechanic with the truck asked him what was wrong with the car, Thompson said that he had no idea.

Frowning his impatience, the mechanic checked under the hood. "Looks and sounds great to me, pal," he said after a few moments' inspection.

"Well, I'm *not* driving it," Thompson said resolutely.

The mechanic gave him another frown. "It's your money."

After the mechanic hitched the bumper to the hoist and lifted the front of the car off the ground, Thompson got into the cab of the truck.

The tow truck had moved no more than five feet when the two men heard a loud crash behind them. The mechanic slammed on the brakes and they jumped out of the cab.

There, on the pavement, lay the front wheel of Thompson's car. It had simply fallen off the axle.

Without saying another word, the mechanic picked up the wheel and put it in the back of the truck. The two men drove in silence back to the garage.

THE DINNER THAT his friend's wife had prepared was quite cold by the time Thompson arrived. He could only offer the excuse of car trouble. He made no effort to tell the couple about the angelic guardian who had once again saved his life.

But he knew that if he had not obeyed his angel's voice, he would most assuredly have had an accident. Not only might he have been killed, but he would undoubtedly have brought injury and perhaps even death to others on the busy freeway.

In the May 1955 issue of *Fate* magazine, Thompson expressed his gratitude to the unseen guardian who saved his life on two separate occasions. And he added: "I advise anyone who may be visited by . . . another of his kind to heed his voice. Do not hesitate to obey his command, no matter how incomprehensible it may seem. You may not be given another chance."

Missouri

ANGELS GAVE HIM THE STRENGTH TO TRIUMPH OVER CHILDHOOD ABUSE

Howard Guthrie told us that angels came to him when he was a child in rural Missouri and gave him the love and support necessary to withstand terrible abuse.

He remembered that he was about five years old when—for some reason he was never able to determine—he became the official physical scapegoat for the other members of his family. Whenever anything in their lives went wrong, Howard was beaten in an almost ritualistic manner by both of his parents and his two older brothers.

One night, when he was about eleven, his father whipped him into unconsciousness for no special reason and left him lying on the ground in back of the corncrib.

"When I awoke, it was dark and I was looking up at the stars," Howard said. "Since we lived out in the country and we didn't have any yard light to mask out the stars, it was like I could see straight up into Heaven. I started to cry, because I really wanted to go home to Heaven that night. I was in a lot of pain because Pa had whipped me so hard. I was lying on the soft, cool grass, and I knew that if I went into the house and up into the room I shared with my brothers, they would probably beat up on me and make me sleep on the floor. So I just lay there, and I started to pray for God to send some angels to come and take me away."

In his childish reasoning, Howard believed that if he just willed himself not to wake up in the morning, he would be dead and God would have to send angels to claim his soul.

"I started noticing seven unusually bright stars moving around the sky, and then I saw that they were coming closer and closer to me. They stopped about twenty feet above the apple orchard, then they slowly lowered themselves to the ground and began coming toward me."

Howard insisted that he was not afraid. "I just thought that a merciful God had granted my prayer and sent his angels to bring me home to Heaven."

The seven glowing, pulsating beings formed a circle around Howard as he lay on the grass in the farmyard. They seemed to float, rather than walk, and he could see their beautiful robes moving ever so slightly as they hovered around him and began to sway in a side-to-side motion.

"I heard a strange kind of musical humming sound, as if the angels were singing. And then I noticed that the pain from the whipping was leaving me."

After the physical healing had taken place, the angelic beings started "putting images" in Howard's mind. "It was kind of like they were showing me a really positive, upbeat movie inside my head. I can't remember everything I saw. I just recall that it was all really inspirational and joyful. I started feeling a tingling sensation, and then, I guess, I fell asleep."

When he awakened the next morning, Howard was suffused with a marvelous sense of purpose for his life. He knew that he would withstand the family's cruelty toward him and rise above the demeaning and debilitating effects of their abuse.

Howard said that he received occasional angelic visitations and "mental movies" all through his adolescent years and up until the time he entered military service. Although his family was unchurched and did not possess a Bible, nearly all of his visions were of a spiritual or religious nature.

"Once I had entered military service, I was totally free of my family," Howard told us. "When I was discharged, I entered college and got a degree in education. I've been a teacher now for twelve years. I'm happily married, with two children. I owe my life and my sanity to those angels who formed that circle around my whipped and battered physical vehicle and healed both my body and my soul on that long-ago night of torment."

New Jersey
THE ANGELS HAVE ALWAYS LOOKED AFTER DEBORA

Janet Dean of Wenonah, New Jersey, is certain that her daughter Debora is a special child who is beloved of the angels.

Consider this incredible episode she presents as only one example:

On a late-winter afternoon in 1993, two-year-old Debora ran ahead of Janet as they entered a second-floor bedroom. The exuberant child ran across the room, jumped up on a chair in front of an open window—and fell out.

Janet's absolute and total horror was immediately transformed into amazement when she beheld her little girl being transported *backwards* into the room.

Later, after her nerves had calmed down to some degree, Janet reflected that the experience was like seeing a motion picture film projected in reverse. She could remember screaming for help—and then, just as quickly as little Debora had fallen out of the window, she came flying back in.

None the worse for what could have been a fatal fall, Debora stood in front of Janet and greeted her with a cheery, "Hi, Mommy," just as if nothing unusual had occurred.

"There is no doubt about it," Janet said. "It was Debora's guardian angel who caught her and carried her back inside. I picked her up in my arms and cried with relief."

Janet believes that angels have always looked after her daughter. "Once, Debora put her foot through a glass door. It shattered, but there wasn't a single cut on her."

New Mexico
GOD SENT AN ANGEL WITH MUSCLES TO LIFT A CAR OFF A TEENAGE BOY

In August 1987, seventeen-year-old Ray Santos of Las Cruces, New Mexico, was repairing the transmission of his 1978 Chevrolet in the backyard of his home when the car slipped off the jack and pinned him.

A steel cross-brace under the steering column pressed heavily and agonizingly against his chest. The pain was unbearable. He felt as though the very life was being crushed out of him.

He tried to take a deep breath, but he couldn't. And every time he shouted for help, he let air out of his lungs—and the terrible weight on his chest increased.

The last thing that Ray remembered before he blacked out was asking God to forgive his sins.

THE SANTOSES' NEXT-DOOR neighbor, sixty-six-year-old Felicita Madrid, heard the boy's faint cries for help as she worked in her kitchen. When she looked out of her window and saw a pair of shoes sticking out from under the Chevrolet, she knew that someone was being killed. Her shouts brought Ray's mother Estelle; another neighbor, Roberta Gavarette; and Roberta's eleven-year-old daughter, Rita.

Estelle Santos cried out in an anguished prayer for Mother Mary and God the Father to send a miracle. "Please help us lift the car off Ray before he dies!"

And then, realizing that they had no time to waste watching the heavens for a sign of comfort, the two women and the girl began trying their best to lift a three-thousand-pound automobile off the unconscious teenage boy being crushed to death by its relentless bulk.

It was when they were about to try again at the count of three that the stranger ran up to them.

"He was not an especially tall man," Estelle Santos recalled later. "But he was stocky and powerfully built.

There was something about him that was kind of strange, fierce, and wild—but his brown eyes were kind."

The stranger wedged himself between the women. "Let me give you a hand!"

Estelle Santos counted to three again. "And when we lifted the bumper, the big man's muscles bulged—and the car rose completely off the ground. It now seemed as light as a feather."

The powerful stranger told Felicita and Rita to pull Ray out from under the car while he and the other two women held the car off his chest.

In the next few minutes of excitement, the ambulance arrived to take Ray to the hospital, and the stranger with all the muscles disappeared.

The teenager was very lucky and, miraculously, suffered no broken bones or internal injuries. He was thankful to be alive, but was upset that his mother hadn't gotten the stranger's name so that they could thank him properly.

LATER THAT NIGHT, Felicita Madrid startled the others when she said that she thought she had finally recognized the man who had appeared out of nowhere to help save Ray's life.

Twenty years before, she told her neighbors, a powerfully built man named Emilio Sanchez had lived in the

Santos house. Sanchez had wrestled professionally for many years, and Felicita recalled the night that he was killed in an automobile accident.

"He was a gentle giant," Felicita said. "Emilio truly loved people—especially children and young people. He was always there to help when he was needed. I believe his spirit returned today to help rescue Ray."

Estelle Santos listened carefully to her neighbor's explanation for the sudden appearance and disappearance of the stranger with the strength of a Samson.

"The important thing is that God heard our prayers and spared my son's life," she said. "Whether he sent us a spirit from beyond or an angel from Heaven, he granted us a miracle by sending us a powerful helping hand."

New York
THE FARMER'S SON WHO TALKED WITH AN ANGEL AND FOUNDED A WORLDWIDE RELIGION

Joseph Smith had always been devout; but it is unlikely that on the evening of September 21, 1823, he was expecting the glowing angel that appeared before him in the family farmhouse outside of Palmyra, New York. Eighteen-year-old Joseph had been in his bedroom, kneeling in prayer, when he was visited by a magnificent being that bathed the room in brilliant light.

Dressed in a splendid white robe, the angel identified itself as Moroni, a messenger from God. "You have been chosen to accomplish many great and wonderful deeds," the heavenly entity told the teenager.

Joseph didn't really want to accept the responsibility of "accomplishing great and wonderful deeds." But as the wide-eyed lad watched, the angel disclosed the place where a book written on gold plates had been hidden.

These plates, according to the angelic messenger, were inscribed with a writing that Joseph would find very strange. Once deciphered, however, they would reveal the account of a prehistoric civilization that had once existed on the North American continent.

"And how," Joseph asked, "can anyone translate and decipher a language unknown to any living person?"

Joseph was shown two strange stones, and the angel told him to look into them. Joseph was amazed to perceive a translation of the ancient writing appear on the surface of the two crystalline rocks.

Moroni manifested three times that night. The next morning, Joseph awakened feeling confused by the extraordinary events that the angel had brought into the life of a very ordinary farm boy.

The young man remained silent about his experience and went about his work as if nothing were troubling him. Later that day, however, as he was plowing a field on the family farm, Joseph slipped into an altered state of consciousness.

As Joseph lay on the newly turned soil, the angel Moroni manifested once again and instructed him to inform his father of the visitations that he had received.

Joseph did as the angel had commanded, and he was encouraged by his father's opinion that he must have been selected to perform great deeds. Thus strengthened, Joseph set out to locate the gold plates. He found them in an Indian burial mound on the farm.

But Moroni materialized once again and instructed Joseph to leave the gold plates in the mound. The young farmer was then told to check on the ancient book once each year to be certain that it was safe.

Joseph did as Moroni commanded. In the fall of 1827, five years after the angel's initial visitation, he was allowed to remove the plates from the mound.

Employing the magical stones according to Moroni's example, Joseph meticulously translated the ancient text to reveal an account of the "Lost Tribes of Israel," those legendary Hebrew people who had allegedly migrated from the Holy Land to settle in ancient America.

———

THE MOST SIGNIFICANT result of Joseph Smith's translation of the golden plates was his founding of the Church of Jesus Christ of Latter-Day Saints, commonly known as the Mormon Church.

From the very beginning, Smith's converts and adherents found themselves in the midst of a stormy religious controversy. While his faithful followers insisted that his *Book of Mormon* was a true revelation from God, other people said that he was just a lonely farm boy seeking fame and fortune. At worst, said the harshest skeptics, it was a sham designed to bilk the gullible; at best, it was a bucolic joke that got out of hand.

In December 1832, Joseph Smith accurately predicted the advent of the Civil War, the tragic conflict that would not begin until April 1861. He also told his followers that they would find their promised land in the western United States—but that he would never see it, since he would die before he was forty.

In the mid-1840s, 148 Mormons began a journey westward to find their promised land. Persecuted and unwelcome wherever they traveled, they paused their trek in the Midwest. In 1844, when he was thirty-nine years old, Joseph Smith was killed by an angry mob in Carthage, Illinois.

In spite of the death of their prophet, the Mormons continued west, eventually ending their journey on the shores of Utah's Great Salt Lake. Today, Salt Lake City is the capital of the Mormon Church's nearly five million members, who believe that an obscure farm boy named Joseph Smith was a true prophet of God who did indeed speak to an angel.

Wales

THE HOUSEWIFE WHO
HEALED WITH ANGELIC BLUE LIGHT

The young mother-to-be was quite distraught, and she expressed her anxiety to the always sympathetic next-door neighbor.

"The doctor says that the baby is not properly placed in the womb," she said. "He says I may have to go to the hospital."

"That would be such a pity," Mrs. Bronwen Evans said softly. It had always grieved her so to see people in anguish and pain. For years now she had been an avowed enemy of suffering. "When do you next see your doctor?"

"Tomorrow," the young woman sighed sadly. "And I'm certain that he'll place me in the hospital then."

"Well, now, don't worry," Bronwen told her. "Nothing is wrong with your baby, my dear. Let's see if we can't give your old doctor a bit of a surprise."

She placed her hands near her neighbor's stomach and moved her fingers in a twisting motion.

The next day, when the expectant mother called upon Mrs. Evans, she was glowing with happiness. She did not have to enter the hospital after all. Everything was as it should be. Her doctor had told her that by "some extraordinary means" the baby had moved to its proper place in the womb.

SOME YEARS AGO, one of our correspondents in the United Kingdom informed us that dozens of folks in the valleys of Wales had discovered that Mrs. Bronwen Evans herself was the "extraordinary means" by which so many miraculous things were occurring. The charming mother of three has been accomplishing astonishing healings through the curative power of her angelic blue light since the closing days of World War II.

Bronwen once told a reporter for the *Herald of Wales* that she had tried for many years to conceal the fact that she was "different" from other people in her town of

Bridgend. As she grew older, she began to realize that strange and wonderful things had happened to her as early as age three.

When she was six, her family had lived next to a woman who used to swear that young Bronwen was continually bathed in a circling blue light sent by the angels.

One day, after her marriage at twenty, Bronwen was approached by a beautiful woman of commanding appearance who told her that it was time for her to begin her healing ministry.

Bronwen was confused and startled by such a command issuing forth from a woman who was a total stranger to her.

Seeking counsel on the matter, Bronwen paid a visit to her mother to tell her of the unusual encounter with the strange woman.

"Perhaps the woman was just some sort of crank," she told her mother. "But I found her words so unsettling, and they seemed to touch something deep inside of me. What if I truly am being guided by angels to perform healing work? What if that truly is my mission here on Earth?"

Her always practical mother suggested that they put the woman's command to the test.

"I have had this lump on my hand for some time now, dear. If you indeed have the gift of healing, make it go away."

Bronwen reached out with trembling fingers to touch the lump on her mother's hand. Consciously, she had no idea what she was supposed to do. But on a deeper level of knowing, something was guiding her, reassuring her.

Then she was suddenly overwhelmed by some nameless energy. A peculiar—yet wonderful—sense of having been suddenly supercharged with some unearthly power surged throughout her entire body.

In a paroxysm of tearful release, she saw that the lump had disappeared from her mother's hand.

She stepped back in amazement, accidentally brushing her mother's head with her fingers. The lump now appeared in the same size and shape on her mother's forehead.

Realizing that she would have to be more careful with this new and awesome gift from the angels, Bronwen reached out to eliminate completely the traveling growth. A kind of bluish-colored energy appeared to emanate from her fingertips—and the lump was gone forever.

ALTHOUGH SHE WAS as astonished as anyone that the mysterious woman had somehow activated her healing abilities, Bronwen began at once to use her new talent to help people in pain and suffering. She had now concluded that the beautiful woman who had appeared so suddenly and had commanded her to begin her healing ministry was probably an angel, rather than "some sort of crank."

Her husband, however, considered both the strange woman and Bronwen's newfound powers to be satanic and dangerous.

But then there was the night when he came home from work with a blinding migraine.

"If you truly have the ability to heal," he challenged her, "cure me of this migraine. I've suffered from these bloody headaches long enough."

Bronwen hadn't really gotten the hang of the healing routine yet, but she felt the same marvelous energy moving into her.

"Somehow my hands were lifted above me without any personal control so that I could focus energy directly into my husband's head. From then on, he suffered no more from migraine headaches."

Bronwen's next patient was a man who had hardly been able to move because of a leg condition. When she arrived at his home, he managed to struggle up from the sofa on which he had been lying and painfully limp to meet her.

She placed her hands on the leg that had been afflicted for so long. She sent the blue angel energy into the precise area of the leg that had given the man so much pain.

Within five minutes, he was able to bend his leg and

walk downstairs, something he had not been able to do before.

From then on, Bronwen Evans could not stop herself. She was soon seeing forty to fifty patients each week.

And, as our correspondent told us, she never accepted a single penny for her angelic power of healing.

Zaire

A CONFLICT OF DARK ANGELS AND ANGELS OF LIGHT

Pastor L. G. Kleckner, a missionary in Zaire (formerly the Belgian Congo), told us of the two teenage girls who were brought to him under the affliction of demon possession. Because he knew that Kamala and Sharja were recent Christian converts, Reverend Kleckner theorized that dark angels might have entered them as a kind of protest against the conversion experience.

He was astonished when he discovered that when the girls were under the control of the negative entities they could understand and speak Latin—a language that normally was totally alien and unknown to them—and each girl could lift extremely heavy loads, well beyond the capacity of two strong men.

Whenever people from the village approached them, Kamala and Sharja would take great delight in embarrassing them by revealing their innermost secrets. Under the control of the possessing entities, the two girls were able to disclose hidden thoughts, fears, and inner desires that no one in a small village would wish his or her neighbors to discover.

When Reverend Kleckner demanded to know the names of the dark angels, they would cry out, "Never! Never!"

One night, in desperation, the pastor prayed that God might send some angels of light to assist him in the great struggle that he had undertaken to exorcise the girls.

Later that same evening, when he resumed the process of prayer to convince the demons to leave the girls, a hoarse voice cried out from somewhere inside Kamala, "Aha, Pastor! I see that you've asked for reinforcements."

Reverend Kleckner said that he could see no angelic bodyguards at his side, but he did feel stronger, more confident. "I guess I will always believe that God heard my prayers for assistance and sent some stalwart members of the heavenly host to back me up," he said.

It was on that same night that finally, after repeated coercion, one of the possessing entities seemed to weaken and stated that its name was Deerhorn.

"It refused to say more when I demanded to know the name of its master," Reverend Kleckner said. "Later, though, the entity used Kamala's big toe to write *Lucifer* in the dirt."

A day or so later, the same entity informed the pastor that he, Deerhorn, was one of the angels that had been cast from the higher world during the great civil war in Heaven. Respecting the authority with which the pastor was conducting the exorcism, the demon asked that, if it should be forced out of the girl, it might receive permission to enter another girl of the village, whom it requested by name.

"Of course I firmly denied such a request," Reverend Kleckner stated, "but I felt that my steady prayers and the reinforcement of the angels of light had so weakened the demons that they were beginning to negotiate. I took this as a sign that they were somehow aware that the time of their possession of Kamala and Sharja was growing shorter."

The dark angel grumbled over Reverend Kleckner's denial of its first request, so it countered with another. Might it then, with his permission, enter the body of an animal?

The missionary once again answered with a solid refusal.

Reverend Kleckner said that he was extremely cautious of every blandishment and threat made by Deerhorn and the other demon, who chose to remain nameless.

"I focused most of my attention on the fallen angel named Deerhorn," the missionary explained. "Although centuries of experience have legislated against accepting the names given by demons as necessarily accurate, exorcists usually find it an advantage in casting out an entity to give it a name, even though the name may be a false one."

On one occasion during their lengthy and exhaustive spiritual duel, Reverend Kleckner sprinkled water from the baptismal font on the demon-possessed teenagers. As the droplets splattered on the girls' flesh, the demons shrieked, complained of being scalded, and begged the exorcist to stop their torture.

By utilizing all the resources of Christian exorcism, Reverend Kleckner at last managed to force the dark angel Deerhorn to leave Kamala.

"Before it accepted its final defeat, the demon dropped Kamala to the floor in great agony," Reverend Kleckner said. "Her face became so swollen that she could not open her eyes. Her body went into convulsions.

"After the violent muscle spasms had ended, the girl remained as motionless as if she were dead. When Kamala finally regained consciousness, Deerhorn, as well as the nameless entity that had gained dominion over Sharja, left and never returned. Fervent prayer, the angels of light, and the power of God had once again triumphed over the minions of darkness and deceit."

Epilogue

*For to his angels he has given command about you, that
they guard you in all your ways.*
—Psalm 91:11

*Every man hath a good and a bad angel attending on him
in particular, all his life long.*
—Robert Burton

It is our true belief that all things work together for good
for those who love God. However, we have been given
free will—and that is the problem. The great difficulty in
all of our lives on Earth is acquiring the *discernment* to
tell the difference between the good and the bad.

We have seen in our research and in our counseling
how many individuals believe they have heard "the voice
of God" or "the voice of an angel" tell them to do things
that turned out to be clearly wrong.

We must always bear in mind that there are good

angels and bad (fallen) angels. So just because we believe that an angel has given us a particular bit of advice, it does not necessarily mean that it is the right thing to do. The Bible reminds us always to "test and try" the spirits and the angels. We must know at all times with whom we are dealing!

The holy books of all traditions around the world teach us that there are millions upon millions of angels with different assignments, capacities, and missions. There are guardian angels, warrior angels, angels of love and light, healing angels, angels of joy, angel record keepers, and so on. We are also told that there are many levels of angels, from those that are just "a little higher" than we, to those angelic beings that surround God and are with him at his heavenly throne.

One of the reasons why the priests and various church fathers may have kept the records of angelic acts away from the masses for such a long time may have been precisely the same as our reason for strongly advising certain cautions now—and that is to avoid "angelolatry," a worship of the angels.

Remember that we humans are just a little lower than the angels. This, according to all holy teachings, means that there may be countless angelic beings with not a great deal more discernment than we have as finite creatures on Earth. While they may indeed have a heavenly purpose and a godly mission, that does not mean that we should ever worship or pray to them—just as we should not pray to a wise or highly spiritual fellow human.

Rather, it is given to us to pray to the one Living God and then trust that our prayer will set in motion the mission of the angels. It is to that end and purpose that we celebrate and honor the beauty of God's holy design together with the care and protection of his couriers, his messengers, the angels.

ABOUT THE AUTHORS

BRAD STEIGER is the editor of *Project Bluebook* and the author of *The Fellowship*. He is also the author or coauthor of one hundred and forty other books that have more than fifteen million copies in print. He and Sherry Hansen Steiger are the authors of *Angels Over Their Shoulders*.

SHERRY HANSEN STEIGER is the author or coauthor of over twenty books. Fomerly on staff at Lutheran School of Theology, she is also a family and crisis counselor, and an ordained Protestant minister.

The Steigers live in Forest City, Iowa.